Full Cycle

Full Cycle

Round the Isles by Bike

Stuart Craig

Lindsay Publications

First published in 2001 by
Lindsay Publications
Glasgow

ISBN 1 898169 26 8

A CIP record of this book is available from the British Library

Designed and typeset in 10/12 Baskerville
by Eric Mitchell, Glasgow

Front cover: Designed by C & R Graphics, Cumbernauld

Printed in bound in Finland by WS Bookwell

CONTENTS

DEDICATION

This book is dedicated to
Julia, Philippa, Fiona and Tony
and to my wife Clare

PREFACE

THIS IS AN ACCOUNT OF TWO JOURNEYS that I took around the Western Isles of Scotland using only the ferries and my bicycle for transport. Both journeys were separate and both were a week long. Separate is the operative word for the two weeks were separated by four years. The first trip in 1995 involved fifteen of the more southerly islands, including the islands of the Clyde. It took me until 1999 to find the time to do the more westerly and northerly islands of the Hebrides. I have stitched the two trips together, as I always intended, to give an account of one long sojourn to the islands with my trusty bike.

I did not always travel alone. During the 1995 trip I met Alexander (Sandy), a school teacher from Renfrewshire. Although our routes that year were different from each other our bicycle tracks kept crossing which added interest and companionship to the trip. Since 1995 we have done a few shorter trips but in 1999 we decided to complete the west coast islands together. The book is not meant as a travel guide, cycle route planner or a shipping almanac but as an account of experiences and encounters as I made my way around the carefully chosen routes. Even if you are not a cyclist the journey may well appeal to you, especially if you have an interest in the west coast of Scotland, the islands and the ferries that serve them.

Within the text I have used the 24 hour clock as this correlates with the timetables used by the ferries. Throughout the account I refer to the main ferry company Caledonian MacBrayne as 'CalMac'.

It may assist the reader to have a map of the west coast of Scotland handy in order to appreciate the road distances and the sea-routes involved.

INTRODUCTION to the 1995 TRIP

I WOULD CONSIDER MYSELF MORE OF A SHIP LOVER than a dedicated cyclist. For years now I have pondered over timetables and taken brief trips up to the West Highlands to photograph the ships and the scenery. Many trips have been planned at home on dark winter evenings, the carpet littered with maps, Caledonian MacBrayne brochures and bus timetables. Most of these trips got no further than the carpet.

Then along came my new mountain bike and a dramatic rekindling of any interest in cycling that I had. I realised that I had the means to get myself from one ferry-point to another and thus link up all of those sailing aspirations.

Back to the sitting-room carpet with new timetables and new ideas. How about a week of cycling and cruising around the islands? How many could I reach? The idea was born, the necessary family consent given and the planning of the first part of my journey that now lies within these pages begun in earnest.

My whole reason for going on such a trip was to write about it. Whether my journey was a success or a disaster I would write about it – as if I were some kind of frustrated Alan Whicker or Michael Palin. The fact that I had never written anything before did not seem to concern me. I would go on my journey and then write about it. Perhaps my grandchildren would be interested. Then I began to question my motives.

Why the islands? What is the attraction, the allure? I suppose I don't really know but the individuality of each of the Hebrides is tangible when you visit them. Their insular nature – you have to get on a ship to get to them – makes them seem that bit more remote than other nice places on the mainland that you can simply drive to. Then as you visit more islands there comes this "collecting" thing, like collecting postage stamps or coins or beer bottles (which I've never done) or photographs of ships (which I do). Islands can be collected or bagged and then boasted about to like-minded travellers or anyone in the pub that will listen to you.

"I've been to Berneray, you know!"

"Oh really – which one?"

Maybe it was none of these things that made me pedal off to the islands. Perhaps I'm just a frustrated globe–trotter who has never globe–trotted due to a lack of time and resources.

As my plans took shape the idea of filling the panniers with all that is needed for a week of travelling in the saddle and then heading off – alone – filled me with great excitement and a touch of apprehension. A sense of freedom, no work, no telephones, no queues, no filling metal trolleys at Safeways, no traffic jams, no–one else to consider but myself. There is the downside as well – no wife and no children for a week (I consider that a down side) and of course I may get to the stage where I can't stand my own company for a minute longer.

But I'm back to the islands again. Glasgow to Carlisle, Land's End to John O'Groats did not have the same magical appeal to me as a week in the Hebrides. And that's it. The islands do have a magical appeal as any-one who visits them, writes about them or paints them will tell you. That appeal was all I needed.

The journey turned out to be a huge success and that was down to two main reasons: the fortuitous weather that prevailed throughout, and the planning. As I was initially going to journey alone and with no back–up from anyone else it was essential that careful plans were formulated and potential problems considered in advance. The planning took the form of three concepts:

the *route*, the *bike and I*, and the *practicalities*

THE ROUTE IN 1995

I AM FAIRLY WELL VERSED ON the numerous ferry routes around the Hebrides, Western Isles and islands of the Clyde. This knowledge helped in the planning of my journey but trying to weave a nautical path around the numerous islands is complex if the journey has to last for only one week. There is no point in being stuck on, say, Colonsay for three days. To reach as many islands as possible in a way that makes each visit purposeful I would have to keep on the move and arrange accommodation at a different place for each night.

I did not set out to break any records as far as the number of islands visited or ships sailed on were concerned. Those feats would be impos-sible to attain without a car. Instead I settled on a route that would have a directional basis without me having to double–back on myself too often. From the three plans that I drew up I settled on the one which seemed best to satisfy all of my self-defined criteria.

I would start on the Clyde and finish at Oban. Sixteen islands seemed the likely final total – the furthest north being Coll. Around twenty-six separate ferry crossings would be involved upon fifteen different vessels of various shapes and sizes.

On one day a week (Wednesday) there is a ship connection from Islay to Oban thus linking the islands of South Argyll with the busy port of Oban itself. I therefore planned my route around a Tuesday overnight stay on Islay. The rest of the week was then worked out up to that day and then from that day. Once at Oban I had a degree of flexibility but decided not to venture to the Outer Isles of Barra and the Uists as too much of my time would be taken up sitting on a ship rather than cycling. There were plenty of islands in the vicinity of Oban to keep me occupied for the remainder of the week.

Some flexibility would be useful in case I encountered any unforeseen problems but, inevitably, there were a few sailings that I simply had to be on if my plans were to succeed. I will let the finer details of my route unfold as I relate my experiences.

THE BIKE AND I

My MOUNTAIN BIKE WAS an inexpensive but reliable Townsend KX 100 with 18-speed gears. I am neither particularly mechanically-minded nor skilled with bikes and I therefore had it well serviced just before my departure. I took some emergency spares with me – just in case – and hoped that I would never need them.

A mountain bike is probably not the best machine for a route such as I had in mind, which was predominantly on tarmac roads, but I liked the solid feel and reliability of my own bike. I was not going to break any speed records but this bike would get me around my route without any problems. In my opinion spending hundreds of pounds on a sophisticated bicycle is just not necessary for a trip such as this.

I had never indulged myself on a trip such as this one before and although I had great faith in my bike I was unsure how I would shape up – I was thirty-seven years old after all and during the course of the week would have to cover over two hundred and fifty miles. I would have to train.

Building up my fitness was quite straightforward and enjoyable. I had no need to be a super–fit athlete but I did want to enjoy the cycling each day without being totally exhausted at the end of it. I needed to be fairly fit as I would have no rest days but would have to be able to embark on a fresh stage of the journey each morning without having tired and painful legs. Furthermore, if I was reasonably fit the risk of injury to muscles would be reduced.

As a guide to myself I trained with the aim of being able to cycle forty miles in a day comfortably. Feeling tired at the end of a day was perfectly satisfactory but I had to be comfortable with that distance.

By cycling a few miles daily and once a week embarking on a twenty-five to thirty-five mile trip I soon found that I was gaining in physical stamina. As my stamina increased I became surprised at how well I could perform on a long cycle. My confidence was also increasing.

As the start of my trip neared I was quite certain that I could cover the ground in the time that I had allotted. Looking back now on these targets they seem easily achievable but in 1995 I had never undertaken such a trip before and I was naturally a bit cautious. I have always held the view that cycling should be enjoyable and not purgatory. I did not want to bite off more than I could chew and find myself pedalling along in some sort of miserable gloom wishing I had never started out.

As fitness increases, cycling up hills becomes much less of a problem. Instead, the enemy of the cyclist is wind, the meteorological kind I mean. Should my week coincide with a strong persisting gale then I could be in trouble. Every hill is finite and the energy spent in climbing it is repaid with the downhill reward. A strong wind can be unremitting and eventually very tiring. I could not plan for such a mitigation arising but by my starting date, 6 August 1995, my bike and I were ready.

THE PRACTICALITIES

WHERE WOULD I SLEEP? What if the bike suffered a puncture? How many pairs of socks would I take with me? These are the "practicalities" and during the planning stage I had to answer those questions and dozens like them.

I booked hotels and guest–houses well in advance, as soon as I knew my route and just hoped that I would arrive there. There was no need to "slum it". After a long cycle ride I wanted to be sure that I had food, a shower and a bed to look forward to, without having to start out and look for them. This turned out to be shrewd planning but it did mean that I had to reach a particular destination each night.

I bought rear panniers for the bike and made a list of what I should bring with me. Then I made another list – deleting half of what was on the first list: the hot–water bottle, thermos flask of coffee and my bed-time reading – the complete works of William Shakespeare.

Clothes were cut down to a minimum. I had cycling shorts and cycling longs, a warm fleece and a waterproof top. Apart from these I only brought one pair of jeans, a few T–shirts and smalls, and a change of footwear. Who cared if I was smelly by the end of the week or even halfway through it.

I brought maps, tools and lights. A notebook, pencils and the all-important camera were thrown in. A few medicinal comforts were included: something for a sore head, something for a sore tummy and a small flask containing something for a painful soul, should I suffer any of these.

I was convinced that being totally prepared on paper would be as essential as being physically prepared and so as one last tool I made up a small card for each day of my journey summarising ferry times, cycling distances, places of interest to look out for and lunch stops. The final entry on each card was the *Devil's Advocate* – the *what if* scenario. Here I listed alternative routes, crossings and a few 'phone numbers – just in case. Anyone would think I was setting out to cross the Gobi Desert.

When the journey was completed I could look back at the success and know that it was due in large measure to the planning.

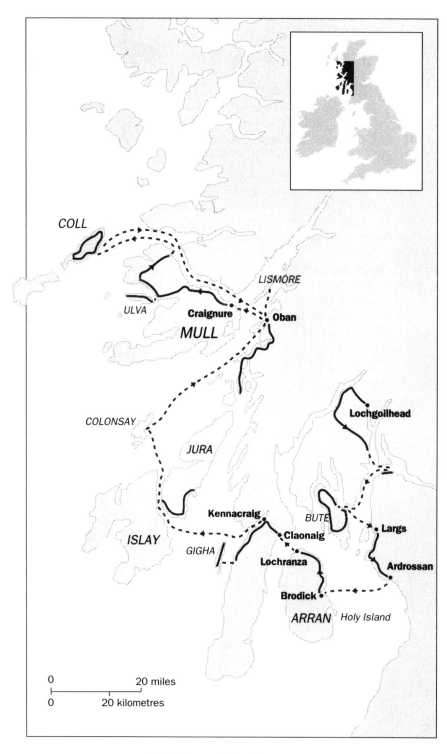

1995 Map of First Journey
Start: Lochgoilhead *Finish*: Oban

DAY 1 – LOCHGOILHEAD TO BUTE

WHY LOCHGOILHEAD? I HEAR YOU ASK. An unusual starting point. Well a holiday for my family at Lochgoilhead was the price of a week of cycling freedom for me, and a fair deal I considered that to be. I would spend a day with them and then commence my trip from there. Starting at Lochgoilhead, deep in Argyll, did present me with one or two difficulties. It meant much timetable-scanning and an early start on Day One of the journey but it could certainly lead to an interesting day, albeit a long one.

I have long considered Loch Goil itself to be the most beautiful loch on the Clyde and the Argyll region a favourite haunt of ours – especially on busy Bank Holiday Mondays when roads to Ayrshire and Loch Lomondside are choked with traffic but the sea routes to Argyll beckon the day-tripper to quiet hills, beautiful still lochs and peaceful woodlands. I am sounding like a tourist guide already.

Lovely as Lochgoilhead may be I had to find my way out of it and the only option that would allow a bike involved a steep climb through the valley named somewhat alarmingly on the map as *Hell's Glen*. While Clare and the children settled themselves into the holiday chalet which was to be their home for the week I tinkered with and pampered my bike and panniers, getting them ready for the week of toil and abuse which they and I were about to endure. I packed and re-packed my two rear pannier bags in an effort to reach a state of complete and total preparation.

I was going to travel light. Although I would be away for seven days I only intended taking five days of clothes with me. I would have to wash some essential items while at one of my overnight stops and hope they would be dry by the morning.

For the bicycle I brought along a few emergency spares that I hoped would never be required: a pump, puncture repair kit, tyre-levers, spare inner-tube, spare chain link, shifting-spanner and pliers. My bike had a good track record, literally, with no problems on the 1500 miles that it had clocked up since its purchase, so I was fairly optimistic that with careful handling I would escape mechanical disasters.

Being a connoisseur of Ordnance Survey maps I had amassed several sheets to cover every part of my journey. I have always found that an OS map adds much valuable information and fun to a long cycle trip. When I counted the maps I needed there were ten. When I felt the combined weight of them I knew I would have to be ruthless, at the risk of getting lost, and cut down on them. I whittled the ten down to six, discarding maps of Bute, Arran, Islay and Tobermory. The remaining six sheets I just had to take with me. They were indeed to prove essential.

Front panniers were not required, I could easily get all that I needed for my trip into the two rear pannier bags. Remaining space on the bicycle tubes was decorated and adorned with the pump, U-lock, lights, water-bottle and 'bum' bag, tailored to fit neatly around my seat post. In this I kept my few valuables and a small teddy bear given to me by my youngest daughter Fiona as a lucky mascot. From now on Ted would stare out of his little pouch as the landscape and seascape receded from him and promote more than a couple of comments from curious fellow travellers. Strangely, as the days proceeded I began somehow to appreciate his tacit companionship. The brain can behave irrationally when one journeys alone.

Tyres were inflated to the correct pressure, new batteries installed in my lamps and my on-board cycling computer set to zero. The bike was as ready as it could be. Was I?

We had our last family meal together – lots of pasta – which nutrition experts tell us is very good for maintaining energy levels (I was to be very particular about what I ate and drank during the trip). I then had one more look at the maps and timetables to finalise in my mind my targets for the following morning.

My first goal of the opening day was to reach Dunoon pier – twenty-nine miles away – by 10.50 in order to catch my first ferry. If I were to fail in this objective the rest of the day's plans would gradually disintegrate. To assist me in reaching Dunoon on time I decided to 'chicken-out' of the early morning ascent of *Hell's Glen*; Clare would drive me plus bike up to the summit of the western approach to Lochgoilhead. Maybe this is considered as cheating. So what! The summit is 219 metres and I considered it an unnecessary burden at the start of my journey – especially when I had a ship to catch and the probability of ruining my day if I missed it. I wanted to conserve my energy resources for later in the day, when I would definitely need them.

From the summit of the glen I anticipated a magical cruise downhill to St. Catherine's on Loch Fyne, four miles away, and then a flat run to Dunoon.

The second essential ingredient to help me to reach my goal was an early start. I would set off early and allow myself two hours and forty-five minutes for the twenty-nine mile cycle.

The summit of *Hell's Glen* at 07.55 on Day One, a Sunday, is a mist-swathed, cloudless scene with temperatures cool enough to necessitate the wearing of a fleece over my T-shirt.

A disturbed night's sleep due to my excited state of mind and the noisy antics of some lager louts outside our chalet has left me with a rather numbed vein of emotions as I bid farewell to Clare and the children. All going well, I will see them in a week upon Oban pier. If it all goes wrong I'll be back in time for supper.

The car recedes downhill towards Lochgoilhead and the sound of its engine fades. Peace returns to the glen and I sit there, at the top, poised upon my saddle, front wheel pointing downhill, my heart thumping in anticipation of not only the descent which curls its way before me but of the week of cycling adventure which lies ahead. At this moment I feel very vulnerable. I've never done anything like this before and right now it seems as though the whole of the west coast of Scotland lies before me.

Months of planning have gone into my trip. Here now, at this very moment, it is about to begin.

A meadow pipit tweets indignantly at me from a nearby fence post and brings me back to my senses. I've been sitting here for five minutes – am I going to go or not ! I'm off.

The ride down to the shores of Loch Fyne is exhilarating. The cool early morning air rushes in my ears and I have to work at restraining the heavy, loaded bike from flying off the narrow single-track road. I am not expecting any on-coming traffic but cannot ignore the possibility of a car rushing up the hill towards me. I meet nothing.

I am neither an experienced nor a particularly daring downhill racer and on a steep winding road like this one I tend to be rather cautious. There is a whole week of fun ahead of me and I don't want to risk bike or limb on the first two miles. My eyes only leave the tarmac once, to follow the flight of a pair of bullfinches that flutter into the trees ahead of me.

When I join the main road that skirts the eastern shores of Loch Fyne I am able to relax and let the bike go. By the time I reach St. Catherine's I have four miles behind me and have hardly touched the pedals. I give it all I can in the highest gear and am above 30 mph by the time the road levels out.

It is an easy cycle to the village of Strachur and I stop at the road junction there for a quick munch at a roll. Only forty-five minutes have elapsed since *Hell's Glen* and I have covered ten miles. I've made three stops: once to take my sunglasses off, once to put them back on again and once to shed my fleece – which I am not to need when cycling for another six days!

On past the mirror waters of Loch Eck. With the aid of my computer I reassure myself that I am well on schedule. My average speed is above my conservative estimate and I decide to stop for a ten minute break when I reach the small caravan site at the southern end of the loch.

During my training for the trip I found it useful to stop regularly for a quick snack to help keep the energy levels high. Bread rolls are the perfect food for me and after many experiments with drinks I consider natural fresh orange juice the ideal energy source and thirst quencher. I make it a rule-of-the-road that each time I stop, for whatever reason, I will take a slurp from my bottle. Regular pauses, even just for a minute or two, for a quick drink or half a roll before I feel thirst or hunger become an important part of my cycling regime. I always carry plenty of carbohydrate foods and extra drinks with me. Running short of fuel on a long cycle ride has a disastrous effect on a rider's performance, irrespective of how fit he or she is. On this first leg of my journey I have four filled rolls with me and have consumed them all by the time that I reach Dunoon.

At the side of Loch Eck I chat to a chap tending his boat at a small jetty a mere six metres from the roadside. We marvel to each other about the scenery, the warmth of the sunny morning and the relaxed holiday mood that ensues when both coincide. He and his wife have searched the length and breadth of Scotland for "their perfect caravan site" and chosen this one at Loch Eck. On a beautiful morning such as this I could not argue with their choice.

I set off again, now only ten miles from Dunoon and feeling very relaxed in the knowledge that barring a major catastrophe I will easily make my ferry connection. Any earlier anxieties or doubts to the contrary are now dispelled and I pedal with a bit less urgency. I am in no rush and I know that by noon it is going to be hot; there is a lot more cycling to be done beyond Dunoon.

I reach the Holy Loch where the American Naval presence is now conspicuous by its absence. For most of my life the huge US mothership dominated the small sea loch but now the only sizeable presence upon the water are the vessels of Western Ferries whose newly acquired *Sound of Scalpay* is in active service while *Sound of Shuna* lies moored to Ardnadam pier. The *Sound-of-something-else* is tied up at Kilmun pier on the other side of the loch.

I take the coastal route via Sandbank and Kirn and at 10.31 arrive at Dunoon pier. I feel very pleased with myself and celebrate with another slurp of orange juice. An interesting afternoon doon the watter lies before me now.

The ferry which I have toiled to catch is Caledonian MacBrayne's *Juno* which is operating on the Dunoon to Gourock service. I am in possession of a Rover ticket that will allow my machine and me eight days of unlimited travel on CalMac's fleet of ships. It is excellent value for money and means that I don't need to buy a separate travel ticket each time I board a ship.

At 10.50 precisely the *Juno* slips sideways away from Dunoon pier with the aid of her Voth-Schneider propulsion units, and the bike, Ted and I are off across the sea upon the first of the many vessels which are to play a part in my little Hebridean adventure.

I sit out on the upper deck of the ship with a polystyrene cup of tea and watch a three-year-old boy perched precariously on the deck rail, his tummy balancing on the top. His mother chats nearby to a friend, totally oblivious of his actions. She isn't watching and three or four minutes later I can't bear to watch either. I move off downstairs.

Get chatting to the purser about the glorious weather and how the numbers of tourists and day-trippers are flourishing.

"We took 4,000 passengers over to Dunoon yesterday!" he boasts. He is pleased that the ships are busy but my concern is that I will get a ticket for the *Pioneer*'s cruise from Largs to Brodick the following day. She is a vital link in my journey and I have heard rumours that she has been sailing almost full on some days.

"Buy a ticket for the cruise *today* at Largs ticket office and you should be all right," the purser reassures me. If I fail to get on that ship tomorrow I will have to do some serious re-thinking about my itinerary so I take his advice onboard.

I pedal off at Gourock and quickly set out for Greenock where I will hopefully pick up the paddle-steamer *Waverley* for the next link in the chain. As you realise the ships are just as important as the bicycle.

It is rather disorientating cycling along the cycle-path on Greenock Esplanade towards Custom House Quay. Surely I am heading in the wrong direction? It is a minor detour no less and I arrive at the quay a full half hour before *Waverley* is due to berth.

Custom House Quay has recently been landscaped and generally tidied up. It is now a smart embarkation point for that grand old steamer. A few dozen prospective passengers are hanging around in the midday sunshine awaiting the thump-thump of her paddle wheels which would herald her arrival. Having been out in the sun for four hours now I find the heat of the sun reflecting off the flagstones of the quay is sapping my energy and retire to the shade to await the paddler's arrival.

Much has been written on the last sea-going paddle-steamer in the world and I do not intend to go into any detail on her for the purpose of illustrating my journey. Suffice it to say she is a grand old ship, very dear to a Glaswegian's heart, especially mine. What a pity more of her kind could not have been saved from the indignity of the breaker's yard. In my memory I can recall trips on the *PS. Caledonia*, the second last Clyde paddler, and on the turbine steamers *Queen Mary II* and *Duchess of Hamilton*. The *Waverley* is now all that is left. A real ship, the epitome of a living, working museum. I was fond of the *Queen Mary II* but from a purely personal point of view the *Duchess of Hamilton* had that perfect shape and form that for me made her aesthetically the perfect Clyde Steamer.

It is to the great credit of those who had the foresight to save the *Waverley* and those who now run her that she is still here for the next generation of passengers to enjoy. Having recently had a few hundred thousand pounds spent on her in order to satisfy the latest round of Department of Transport regulations, money raised solely from enthusiasts and passengers, she now looks better than ever. Whenever I see her paddling onto a pier I get a thrill tinged with a little nostalgic sadness. My late father employed himself in some volunteer carpentry during the early years of her ownership by the preservation societies. He loved her and I know a fair bit of that affection has rubbed off on me. A little part of him still seems to be aboard her.

Today *Waverley's* decks are crowded with six hundred passengers and her purser is smiling. The bike gets hoisted aboard and we lie alongside until the designated departure time of 12.10. As we prepare to cast off three women can be seen running up the quay. The purser spots them.

"Are you sailing with us?" he shouts. Their run slows to a trot and they shake their heads. The purser shrugs and pulls the gangway onboard. "Why not?" he adds.

I sit back and relax in the now powerful sunshine. Doon the watter to Rothesay on the *Waverley*, a real delight and wonderful to be able to include her in a journey such as this one.

Our route today will take us to Largs and then across the Firth to Rothesay where I will leave the ship and take in my first island, Bute. The paddler will continue without me up to Dunoon and then cruise, ironically, to Loch Goil. She will then retrace her wake and I will catch up with her later on. What a pity Loch Goil Pier is no longer in use (the last steamer to call there was the *Maid of Skelmorlie* in July 1965), I could have jumped on there and saved myself a lot of cycling.I lean over the starboard deck rail listening to the paddle floats striking the water. Something seems different. The usual rhythmic beat (to which I am fairly accustomed being a regular passenger) sounds strangely discordant today. This is not her normal cadence. There is a note missing. An enquiry is made, for I am a very nosy person, and it transpires that a couple of days previously a paddle float had struck some floating debris and been damaged. This has altered her usual harmonious duet with the waves. My ears are not deceiving me.

Largs pier is crowded with day-trippers. A couple of hundred people await the *Waverley* while a similar number queue for the Cumbrae ferries. It is like one of those crowded scenes from the heyday of the Clyde Steamer. Millport, capital of the Island of Cumbrae, is hosting a Country and Western festival and with the bonus of unremitting sunshine it is going to be a very busy little town today. I am planning to pay it a visit later in the day – the crowds cramming onto the ferries should be sending the alarm bells ringing, however.

When we berth at the pier at Largs I hand over my pannier bags to my niece Carolyn who stays in Largs and has come down to the pier to meet me. This will allow me to cycle *light* on Bute. I instruct her to get

me a ticket for the popular *Pioneer* cruise, as advised. I would be returning to Largs on *Waverley* later in the afternoon and then join one of the
overworked ferries for my visit to island number two – Cumbrae.
Meanwhile, the paddler turns her bow towards the island of Bute and
off we sail again, splashing across the dazzling blue sea.

The popular car sticker embellishing the rear windows of Rothesay
tourists proclaims: *Bute Is Beautiful* and it surely is. It is a tranquil,
verdant island with soft contours, rolling bracken covered hills in the
north and a volcanic plug of rock forming its southern headland,
known as Garroch Head.

Garroch Head, to anyone who knows the Clyde, is infamous as the
destination of the "sludge-boat" which brings treated sewage down river
from Glasgow and dumps it into the sea a mile or two from the tip of
the headland. Even the sludge-boat is called *Garroch Head* and can be
seen sailing down river daily, low in the water, with its undesirable but
bio-degradable cargo. She even takes an institution-full of OAPs down
with her, just for the sail, but she always manages to bring them back.
Lunch is served without even a whiff of what unmentionables lie below.
Those on Bute, however, need not be alarmed; the river, tide and what
fish are left carry the 'do-ings' far out into the Atlantic and the shores of
the island are left unsullied.

The middle of the island is rich farming country. There are dozens
of farms on Bute. And hundreds of cows! They leave their mark on the
road and the dictum is: don't wash your car before you take it over to
Bute but book it in for a five star valet on your return.

Today I am in Rothesay, a smashing wee town but somewhat down
on its luck in recent years. The rows of empty shops on the front provide testament that times are hard for many in the community.

The Winter Gardens, venue of many a variety performance, was
reopened a few years ago after considerable alluring refurbishment.
Sadly during the first winter of its rebirth the Clyde flooded due to a
combination of heavy weather and a high spring tide. The Winter
Gardens and the pier were submerged. That day CalMac could
have sailed their *Saturn* up Montague Street. In the event the ferry
lay off out in the expanding bay until the pier re-emerged from the
waves.

A few years ago I stood on the starboard deck of the same vessel as
she set off from Wemyss Bay towards Rothesay into the teeth of a force
eight gale. The captain pointed the bow of his ship south towards Largs,
into the storm as part of an altered course. After a few minutes a fellow
passenger dressed in baggy, beige flannel trousers and tweed jacket
swung his head around from his position overlooking the bow to
enquire of me: "Is this ship *going* to Rothesay?"

"Yes," I replied – and then sounding like a real smart Alec added,
"She's heading south into the gale but will soon swing around to be

carried with it into Rothesay." (I had been here before!) "I wouldn't stand out there if I were you, it's a bit exposed."

The chap merely smiled and remained where he was. A brief moment later a wave crashed over the upper deck and the flannel trousers and tweed jacket were duly drenched. He looked as though someone had thrown a bucket of water at him and he submissively nodded as he waddled off downstairs like a child who had been caught short. The wry smile was now on my face.

There is a strange riddle about another form of transport on the island. Until a few years ago nearly all the taxis on Bute were Ladas. Did the local council have some mutually acceptable contract with the Russian manufacturers of the car? The trend certainly seems to have died along with the collapse of the Soviet Union.

Rothesay is known as the Madeira of the Clyde and on this glorious Sunday afternoon its Atlantic cousin could not have been any hotter than the Clyde resort. Many Glaswegians still flock to Rothesay and it is the most popular destination for *doon-the-watter* trips on the *Waverley*.

When I was a lad in the 1960s it was the car-ferries *Cowal* and *Bute* that transported us for our annual Easter holiday, although I remember some of the other visitors to the pier, like the *Waverley* or *Queen Mary II* or one of the *Maids* such as the *Maid of Skelmorlie*.

Hundreds, including myself and bike, now flood ashore to join in the revelry. I do not consider myself a holiday-maker or day-tripper. My three and a half hour visit has to be a purposeful one.

I have allowed myself the liberty of two choices: I can either cycle a ten-mile circuit in the centre of the island, taking in Ettrick Bay on the west coast, or I can visit the recently re-opened Mount Stuart House in the south.

Mount Stuart was until recently Bute's best kept secret. Set in extensive wooded parkland in the south-eastern corner of the island it is the home of the Marquis of Bute and was never seen by the public until the surviving Lady Bute magnanimously decided to open the house and gardens as a tourist attraction in June 1995.

I have always known of the existence of the house and indeed have glimpsed its red sandstone structure through the trees from offshore. But when I visited with my family in June nothing could have prepared me for the outstanding beauty of the gardens and the fabulous architecture of the house itself.

A multicoloured marbled atrium forms the centre-piece of a fascinating and exquisitely designed building. The third Marquis was largely responsible for the style and characterisation of his home. Astrological features and humorous effigies abound and the effect is fantasy of an almost subliminal quality. A real *Alice in Wonderland* house. The greatest mystery was how such a building could remain an enigma on the small island of Bute for so long.

As I have visited the house only recently, I decide, for the purpose of my journey, to set off on the ten-mile cycle. With the sun so hot the prospect of a dip in the sea at Ettrick Bay is too tempting.

Until the 1950s tramcars used to run from Port Bannatyne, Rothesay's neighbouring village, to Ettrick Bay four miles away across the island. The course that it ran can still be seen on the left hand side of the road.

Now cycling light I take the shore road through the Port where I spent most of the Easter holidays. I pass the old pier, once the calling point of many a steamer but now in an advanced state of decay. The last steamer to sail away from Port Bannatyne was the *PS Jupiter* in September 1939.

The road swings inland between the playing field where I used to kick a ball around and the bluebell wood where my parents had romantic moments during their courtship in the late 1930s – so they told me. A short cycle and I have arrived on the other side of the island at Ettrick Bay.

The vista at Ettrick Bay reminds me of an old Victorian postcard scene. The beach is crowded with people and maw, paw and the weans are paddling up to their knees in the sea. I cannot recall having seen the beach as populous before. Everyone seems to be having such a good time – so much so that I decide I am going to have to join them.

I find a chap with an honest face who does not look as though he is going anywhere in a hurry and ask if he can keep an eye on my bike. Shoes and socks off and I too am paddling up to my knees. Despite the proximity of the aforementioned Garroch Head the water is crystal clear and, surprisingly, not cold. I don't mean warm, I mean *not cold*! It is very refreshing on my hot feet. A brief notion enters my head – I could cancel my trip and spend the week here!

Fifteen minutes later I am on my way again continuing along the track behind the beach to rejoin the road. A pleasant cycle follows, towards Rothesay, completing the circle. I come upon a road sign which points in all directions to *Rothesay.*

Of the many islands of the Clyde estuary and Scottish west coast that I have visited Bute remains one of my favourites. Despite its proximity to Glasgow it is easily accessible and one can find a deserted beach within two hours of leaving the big city. The beaches are certainly not deserted today but the island and its rolling landscape still retain a serenity and a tranquil, unassuming beauty. These are features that I feel I am going to encounter many times in the days to follow.

The west coast of Bute has some fascinating spots such as St. Blane's Church, the pencil thin promontory of St. Ninian's and Stravannan and Dunagoil Bays. I want to visit them all but I only have an hour and a half left before the *Waverley* returns to paddle me away to new adventures.

Racing downhill into Rothesay my speedometer touches thirty-five miles per hour. Not exactly a cycling speed record but fast enough for me on my mountain bike and I am, of course, breaking the speed limit!

In Rothesay town I pay a visit to a well-frequented hostelry owned by a relative of mine, Robin Patrick. With the bulk of my cycling over for the day, I have clocked forty-five miles so far. I consider that I deserve a refreshing pint and a bit of Robin's merry chatter.

He is well familiar with the "Big Hoose" at Mount Stuart. Robin is a keen bagpiper and a few months ago he and another twenty pipers were invited along to rehearse for a display that they were to give to Lady Bute. They were ushered down to the cellars and instructed, "Don't make too much noise lads the Lady is in residence today!"

I move on to Craigmore Point, past the magnificent Victorian mansions, built by and resided in by the commercial lords of industrial revolutionised Glasgow who commuted by steamer to the city.

The sun still has me reaching for the factor 6 lotion as I lie on the grass. Just offshore a pair of gannets are diving into the sea between the passing ferries *Pioneer* and *Saturn*. I jump back onto the bike and follow the latter to the pier. There I watch as CalMac's first lady skipper skilfully edges the ship alongside. *Waverley* is next in at the pier and I sail off on her having spent a delightful three and a half hours on island number one.

We are now heading across the Firth to Largs where I will leave the old ship. She would head back up river leaving me to cross over to Cumbrae and cycle down to Millport.

I gaze mesmerised at the triple expansion engines for the last time and then drag my tired legs back on deck to prepare my bike for disembarking. Both *Waverley* and myself have had a good day but both of us still have some work to do before we can tie up for the night.

Once off the ship, however, I can foresee an immediate problem. The hundreds, indeed thousands, of people, cars and bikes that had earlier been crowding Largs pier in order to cross to Cumbrae are now queuing on the other side trying to get back to the mainland. The two small ferries, *Loch Linnhe* and *Loch Striven* are struggling to cope and it looks as though their crews are in for some overtime.

I am tired, it is after six o'clock and a study of the growing queue over on Cumbrae makes me decide, fairly quickly, that I would be mad to cross over at this time. Getting over would be easy, getting back tonight would take forever – and might even prove impossible. Cumbrae will have to wait until the morning. I do not have to leave Largs, on the *Pioneer* to Brodick, until 10.40 tomorrow so I will have plenty of time then to have a quick trip over to the island.

Largs has that striking continental look which it often has on hot, balmy nights when the main street and promenade are crowded.

Everyone strolling about tonight seems to be shirt-sleeved or summer-frocked and either bronzed or burnt by the sun. I watch *Waverley* paddle away – the sing-songs aboard have not yet commenced. I set off to find my accommodation, happy with my decision but blissfully unaware that problem number two awaits me.

I am staying overnight in Largs with my brother Stephen and his family. They greet me with the news that the cruise to Brodick by *Pioneer* the next morning is fully booked. The ticket allocation for Largs has been used up. I flop into the shower to consider what this means to my trip and what I am going to do now. A major change of plan and cancellation of my planned early morning visit to Cumbrae is immediately obvious. I will now have to catch the morning sailing from Ardrossan to Brodick instead of the Largs to Brodick trip. I would have no problem getting onto the Ardrossan ship. For the rest of the day's itinerary to work I simply *had* to be on Arran by midday. If not, my whole day would fall apart.

Instead of sailing from Largs to Brodick direct by the cruise ship *Pioneer* my route to Arran would be by means of an early train to Ardrossan and the service vessel *Caledonian Isles* to Brodick. I could queue on Largs pier at 09.00 for the chance of a cancellation ticket for the *Pioneer* but I could not risk failure. I am disappointed. It is only day one and I have missed an island already – all because of a folk festival and a highly successful cruise. It cannot be helped.

I am disappointed at missing Millport. A delightful small town where, for me, the sun never fails to shine.

During the planning of the trip I had been keen to visit the three main islands of the Clyde. Bute has been a success but given the choice between Cumbrae and Arran the latter is essential to the advancement of my itinerary and that has to take precedence.

Day One = 48 miles

Footnote: Later in the week I learned from a CalMac representative that on this particular Sunday the ferries carried 9,500 passengers over to Cumbrae – beating the previous record by 1,000.

DAY 2 – ARRAN & GIGHA

MONDAY COMMENCES WITH MORE BLUE SKIES and at 08.00 the temperature is already very pleasant. I am standing outside the CalMac office in Largs hoping that the helpful lady behind the counter can find a place for me aboard the 10.40 sailing to Brodick. If she can then I will be able to dash over to Cumbrae. If not, the bike and I will have to be upon the 08.28 train out of Largs to South Beach, Ardrossan and Cumbrae will sadly have to be missed.

The lady might be helpful and sympathetic but the *Pioneer* has a reduced passenger certificate for this particular route and rules are rules. The ship is full and I decide not to risk waiting for a cancellation, in case it is in vain, and so I am soon standing on Largs Railway Station platform instead.

Station is a bit of a misnomer here. The station building and three shops adjacent to it were demolished by an early morning commuter train with brake problems a few weeks before my trip. Fortunately nobody was seriously injured – had the train been an hour later the story might have had a different ending.

"Why take the train?" I hear you asking critically. The answer is time. I do not have the time to pedal the twelve miles or so to Ardrossan. Quite frankly I don't have the inclination either. It's islands that I want to cycle on.

"The train is running twenty minutes late," the station master announces loudly.

I briefly stop swatting the midges from my arms and legs to check my watch and timetables. No problem. I can afford a twenty minute delay.

As if to appease the dozen or so passengers perched on the bare platform the station master produces two upholstered chairs from his temporary office and carries them over to us."Would anyone care for a seat?"

The train arrives – twenty-five minutes late.

At South Beach station the driver manages to bring us to a halt safely and I immediately set off on the short cycle to the harbour. There, two CalMac ships lie, *Claymore* and *Caledonian Isles*. The former is being utilised at weekends for trips to the Isle of Man but it is the latter that I am due to sail on. The new *Caley Isles* is the largest ferry ever built for Clyde service. She is a fine vessel with ample accommodation – but who gave her that name? Surely the title *Caledonia*, a traditional name for a Clyde vessel, would have been more apt. A personal view!

Waiting on the quayside I look around me in amusement as other cyclists materialise and begin to form a queue in preparation for boarding. First one or two and then another three or four followed by a further six or seven. Soon there are dozens of us. I study their bikes and clothes and am reassured that I seem as well equipped and look as daft as they do. I wonder if they are embarking on as crazy a journey as I am. Perhaps they are just going over for a day trip. By the amount of bags that some of them are carrying they look as though they will be on the road for months. I adjust my goggles and try to look cool.

The bike is securely stored aboard and I ascend to the forward deck to watch the 'entertainment' - namely the amusing spectacle of the late-comers. This is a daily occurrence at most ferry terminals. They will saunter up in drips and drabs and then panic when they discover that they require a sailing ticket from the booking office before they board. The nonchalance evaporates as they rush between ship and booking office and back to ship again. Our sailing time is 09.45 and the car ramps are up when the next flock of late-comers appears in the distance. I think they look comical until I catch sight of my lycra-clad reflection in an Observation Lounge window.

It is while watching all these shenanigans that I first meet Sandy, a school teacher and his son Kenneth, who are also off on a week long island-hopping and cycling trip. Like me, Sandy is hanging over the ship's rail laughing at the comings and goings. He takes a look at me and laughs even louder.

"You look as though you are well prepared for a long trip."

"Appearances can deceive," I reply, and we strike up a conversation and a friendship which forms an important part of the rest of this story. The route that they are taking today is very similar to my own; indeed our paths are to cross several times in the forthcoming days as we weave our individual webs around the Hebrides. Their preparations have been less pedantic and more spontaneous than mine, as I quickly discover when I ask Sandy a few probing questions.

"I've been planning this for eight months – when did you decide to do this?"

"Yesterday," replies Sandy, trying hard to keep his face straight. "My wife Janet said, 'if you're going to go then *GO!*'"

They have no accommodation booked ahead, for instance, and not even a banana between them. When I tell Sandy my plans and counter-plans and alternate plans should my counter-plans not work out – his smile is more blatant, and then his laughter undisguised.

"If my plans go wrong," he says, "I've got no alternatives – I'll just have to go home."

One advantage of crossing to Brodick on this earlier sailing is that I

27

have more time for cycling on Arran. My immediate aim is to get up to Lochranza at the north of the island and catch the 13.15 sailing to Claonaig on the Kintyre peninsula. I know that I can now make that sailing very comfortably, despite the heady 199-metre climb in Glen Chalmadale. I can relax and enjoy my all too brief time on Arran.

I first visited Arran in 1974 and immediately fell in love with the place. It has an atmosphere of its own unique amongst the Scottish islands that I have visited. It is not something that can be easily explained on paper. Arran just has a *feel* to it. In that year I got to know the mountain geography fairly well by doing a fair bit of walking. The following year I was back again and hired a bike. I set off around the 'north circular' route from Brodick to Blackwaterfoot and Lochranza. Unfortunately I did not take enough to eat with me and by the time I reached Sannox on the home leg I was quite hypoglycaemic (sorry – low blood sugar) and giddy. Today I was confident that I was better prepared – for a start I had lots of food with me – which I knew would outweigh the fact that I was also twenty years older.

Numerous holidays and excursions to Arran have followed over the years, sailing over on various ships: *Caledonia, Clansman, Glen Sannox, Iona, Pioneer, Balmoral, Waverley* and *Isle of Arran.* That special Arran feeling still hits me as soon as I walk, pedal or drive off the ferry.

It is still a popular holiday destination, particularly for those who like a bit of the outdoors stuff like walking, golfing, hill-walking etc. Be warned, however, apparently the island is home to the highest density of poisonous snakes in Europe. All adders of course so Sandy should be in good company – he's a maths teacher. (You might have to read that bit again.) As a matter of fact the only time I have seen an adder in Scotland was on Arran, near Fallen Rocks in the north-east. A metre of slinky silver and black slithering into the undergrowth out of my way. I searched for it, very gingerly, to no avail and then had to search for the girlfriend who was with me but had run a mile when I'd shouted *SNAKE!*

Talking of slithery creatures, during my 1974 visit I encountered a rather strange apparition which is worth recalling. Well up Glen Rosa (now *there* is an atmospheric place if ever there was one) in the middle of the gravelly footpath I found a puddle of rainwater containing a foot-long eel. It had just finished raining heavily, as it does on most days in Arran, and there were puddles everywhere. But this one held an eel – and a live wriggly one at that. Now it wasn't an overgrown earthworm and it certainly wasn't a snake but how did it get there – two miles from the sea and one hundred and eighty metres above sea-level? The puddle was less than a metre in diameter. My theory is that it was scooped out of the sea by a water-spout and precipitated down into Glen Rosa by the heavy rain. A few minutes earlier I could have got it down my neck – and then I would have run the mile.

I never cease to be amazed at why people queue to disembark from a ship. Ten minutes before the *Caledonian Isles* docks at Brodick Pier crowds are accumulating in anticipation at the embarkation point on the port side of the ship. They are missing the best bit – watching a ship tie up at a pier is one of life's pleasures, whether one is on the pier or on the ship itself. Sandy, Kenneth and I wait until the last possible moment before descending the decks to be reunited with our bags and bikes.

Today my journey will take me up into that north-eastern corner, amongst the hills, to Lochranza, fifteen miles from Brodick. The first eight miles are a delightful coastal pedal past the grounds of Brodick Castle and along the raised beach to the linear village of Corrie. A bit further on, past Sannox, the road climbs rapidly to 199 metres above sea-level before plummeting down Glen Chalmadale to the northern village of Lochranza. There, another ferry will hopefully take me over the Kilbrannan Sound to Kintyre. Sandy and Kenneth are taking the same route so although we are cycling independently we expect to see each other on the road.

I set off at my own pace and immediately notice that Brodick is much busier with cars than I can ever remember. The bigger the ferry the more traffic is enticed across the water. I am glad to cycle out of the busy town and onto the open road.

At Corrie I pause for a sandwich beside a banner which announces: *A healthy mouth is a happy mouth.* Perhaps Corrie has been invaded by evangelical dentists who are keen to spread the word. I smile to myself as every passing cyclist, without exception, proclaims the words from the banner aloud. I hear them in English dialects, German accents and French intonations. A bit further on, what at first appears to be a flock of suicidal sheep turns out, on closer examination, to be a row of sculpted mooring stones at the end of the jetty, painted to look like sheep. How clever.

Moving on, slowly, I pause again at Sannox to consume a can of sweetcorn. The label boasts twenty-three grams of carbohydrate – that is good enough for me.

Sandy and Kenneth pass. They seem pleased to be overtaking me:

"Oh *we* must be doing well!" I can imagine them muttering. "Look at that guy in the Lycra stuffing his face again – I bet we'll beat him to Lochranza."

Out to sea the *Pioneer,* running behind schedule, is pushing her way towards Brodick. Ironically had I been aboard, her late running would have presented me with problems.

I can't afford to put off climbing this big hill all day so I push on and try to catch up with my two fellow cyclists. The hill is not a major problem, despite the rising temperature and the fully laden bike but I am glad that I had participated in some training for my trip.

The fruit of all my labours is the exhilarating breeze downhill into Lochranza. A couple of chaps on recumbent bicycles are struggling uphill towards me but my work is over, at least for the time being.

At Lochranza the new distillery is shaping up nicely - and the usual shape it is too. Unfortunately it does not open until two weeks after my trip.

A stop for provisions and to send my family a postcard and on to the ferry slip where I join the *Loch Tarbert* for the 13.15 crossing to Claonaig, on Kintyre.

This is an increasingly popular route for cars and bikes as it provides a link from Arran and the Clyde to Islay and the West Highland routes. Onboard I meet up with Sandy again and we pour over maps with a couple of Swedish motorcyclists. Two young lady cyclists from Holland in very snug fitting cycle-shorts join in and by the time we are half-way across the Kilbrannan Sound the party resembles a United Nations summit as we swap itineraries and ambitions for the week ahead. It gives me no solace that my route looks the craziest of all.

The mountains of Arran recede, my time there has been too short but great fun nevertheless. Two islands behind me, many more still to come. As I cycle off at Claonaig, Sandy is still trying to explain what *doon-the-watter* means to the two Swedes. They look bewildered so I leave them all to sort it out bilingually and head off, just a little behind the two Dutch cyclists. Ahead of me now lies a twenty-two mile cycle across the breadth of the Kintyre peninsula and south to Tayinloan where I have the choice of the 17.00 or 18.00 ferry to the island of Gigha. Time is still favourably on my side but I have a couple of reasonable climbs ahead of me before I can relax on the ferry.

An uphill pant follows and then an undulating ride to the road junction at Kennacraig. There the three-pointed road sign reads: Arran Ferry, Gigha Ferry, Islay Ferry. I am turning left towards Gigha but I wait at the road end for the rest of the UN party. At the road junction Sandy and all the other cyclists turn right towards Tarbert and I alone turn left. Tayinloan now lies ahead of me, sixteen miles away. I am likely to meet up again with Sandy and Kenneth on the Colonsay ferry in two days time. They hope to stay overnight in Tarbert and head out to Islay tomorrow – but on a later sailing from me. We bid each other farewell for the time being.

Still more hills and still the sun beats fiercely down. I had packed leggings and waterproofs for the inevitable downpours that would engulf me. My real meteorological problem, however, is the sun. Lavish latherings of lotion are liberally laid on at the frequent stops I make to quench my thirst.

I stop for a longer rest at a lay-by overlooking the still waters of West Loch Tarbert. The first pangs of loneliness that I am to experience several times are creeping up on me. It was all right earlier in the day when I had the company of the other cyclists but now I feel very much on my own. A car pulls in and the occupants, a young couple, get out and, to my delight, amble over for a chat. We compare our respective travel plans for ten minutes and then set off in opposite directions having divulged some of our intimate travel experiences to each other but never to meet again. Did they ever complete their tour of Argyll's tourist attractions? A camaraderie seems to develop between travellers when they meet other lonely hearts. I find throughout my journey that people are keen to stop and talk to me, exchange experiences and swap information. Perhaps the lone traveller is seeking an audience or a few minutes of their fellow creature's time. Maybe the traveller is viewed as less of a threat if he or she does not emerge from a motor car. It could also be that I will simply talk to anyone!

By the time that I reach the picturesque village of Clachan the hill climbing is nearly over. I pause for another drink and to admire the cottages and quaint church which resemble more a Surrey village than a Kintyre one.

At Ronachan Bay the road rejoins the coast and I stop again. No more Clyde, the seas around me now belong to the Atlantic Ocean. I feel that I have travelled quite a distance and yet Largs was only a few hours ago. I sit at the bay for fifteen minutes. Fatigue is just beginning to make its presence felt. I have cycled thirty miles and climbed a total of 500 metres – fully laden and in temperatures that are by now in the eighties. I can feel my legs tired but still have enough energy left in me for the last few miles, it must be due to those twenty-three grams of carbohydrate in the sweetcorn.

The last seven miles to Tayinloan seems attenuated as a head-on wind now adds to my slight weariness in hampering the progress of the bike. I know, however, that I can take my time and will reach the ferry terminal well on target.

At 17.00 the bike and I are aboard the *Loch Ranza* for the twenty-minute crossing to island number three. The tall bearded crewman seems intrigued by my cycle computer. I run through its functions to much headshaking from him. I am equally interested in the handset that he holds which logs, by electronic beam, the number of passengers aboard. Should the vessel sink then the authorities will know how many victims to search for. The electric eye has logged over six hundred passengers today. When we have finished admiring each other's gadgets the ferry sails.

Mrs McSporran at the Gigha Post Office cum-guest-house-cum-village store is very welcoming. She and her husband boast an incredible number of occupations on the island from postman to part-time fireman, shop-keeper, bike hirer, policeman and undertaker. Their most important asset to me, however, at this time, is their shower.

Gigha means God's Island and is a seven-mile long lush little

31

paradise whose surrounding seas are tempered by the relatively warm waters of the North Atlantic Drift (Gulf Stream). Palm trees sprout in unlikely locations and a half dozen sparkling sandy beaches attract an increasing number of visitors each year. But don't put your big toe into the water and tell me that you can feel the warmth of the Gulf Stream. It's still as freezing as ever. Those palm trees must be very sensitive to subtle changes in temperature or else they're kidding themselves on.

I have only once before stepped ashore on Gigha, for a very brief visit, and over the next few daylight hours I am keen to seek out a few spots and discover why the island is so popular.

Refreshed, clean and with my hand-wrung smalls billowing from the McSporran clothesline I retire to the only hotel to sit under yet more palm trees, pretend I'm in the Bahamas and congratulate myself on a superbly satisfying day. My disappointment at having to skip Cumbrae is now behind me and I am well pleased with my progress. In fact I am indulging in what my family call one of my happy moods.

A small boy in the hotel garden obviously understands that I am a lone traveller and comes over to enquire, "Where's your woman?"

"Miles away in Lochgoilhead," I reply, but he fails to understand why I am journeying alone. Can I? He toddles off back to his family.

His question is a poignant one in terms of his observation that I am alone and in the effect it has on me. Now that my mind is not occupied by the cycling I feel just a touch vulnerable. Not in a physical sense, of course, more in an emotional one. I have never really travelled alone before and it is a sobering experience not having anyone to rave to about the scenery or relive the day's events with. Sure enough, as I look around, everyone in the hotel garden is sitting and talking to someone. Everyone except me. But then the young enquirer's father ambles over for a chat and I'm suddenly happy again. I should have been on Gigha yesterday, he argues. A micro-light aircraft landed in a field adjoining the hotel. The couple aboard it had flown over from Edinburgh, skirting to the north of Glasgow to avoid air traffic control.

"You should have seen them taking off," he giggles. "They looked like Mary Poppins."

Gigha is so peaceful. No traffic. No day-trippers now either, as the ferry has completed its last crossing of the day and can be seen making its way southwards across Ardminish Bay towards the mooring at the south pier. From my seat, beneath the palm trees, the *Loch Ranza* looks like a toy. The whole scene seems quite unreal. My only criticism is that the ale that I have clutched in my hand is not 'real' either.

That evening I pedal southwards to the gardens at Achamore. These were cultivated from mature woodland by Sir James Horlick, of eventide beverage fame, who was once owner of the island. Between 1944, when he purchased Gigha and 1962, when the gardens were presented to the National Trust for Scotland, Sir James planted and propagated several rare species of plant around the fifty acre site. Today they are still a splendid display, quite unexpected on a small island like Gigha.

A stained glass window in the church at Ardminish is dedicated to the memory of Sir James, who died in 1972. The island seems to have a lot to thank him for, which cannot be said for many other private island owners, past and present.

I am unable to spend much time in the deserted gardens as a swarm of ferocious midges descend upon me and make me take to the bike again. A lone sparrowhawk circles above the trees. Why can't they eat midges?

At the south pier the *Loch Ranza* is tied up for the night. There isn't a soul in sight and yet everything seems to be open on Gigha. The gardens, the church, even the Vauxhall Astra parked on the pier with windows open and a ten pound note lying on the passenger seat. It would not lie long like that in the Big City – neither would the car. Here on Gigha, its owner knows that both are safe.

Gigha has a tranquillity that only on Kerrera, later in the week, do I experience again. I vow to myself – well who else is there? – that I will return some day with my family.

The northern half of the island can wait until tomorrow and I retire to the hotel bar for my favourite Islay malt. Islay is my target for tomorrow but a Laphroaig is an irresistible nightcap.

Darkness has fallen and a full moon illuminates my path back to my accommodation. One last check confirms that my smalls are drying nicely. I consider that I can safely leave them out overnight. I fall asleep trying hard not to listen to half of a telephone conversation emanating from the kiosk directly below my open bedroom window.

Day Two = 42 miles

Total for two days = 100 miles

DAY 3 – ISLAY & JURA

I WAKE TO SPARKLING SUNSHINE yet again and take a stroll down to the bay before breakfast. The ferry has already commenced her morning schedule and Mr McSporran comes hurtling down the hill in his van with the mail bags, rushing to get the previous day's correspondence on its way to the mainland.

I plan to leave Gigha on the 10.30 sailing - allowing myself an hour or so beforehand to explore the northern half of the island. My most important goal of the day is the 13.00 ship from Kennacraig, on Kintyre, to Port Askaig on the island of Islay. I will be retracing fourteen miles of my route of yesterday afternoon which involves the coastal flat and then some hills. It seems an easy target to reach but it is a crucial one. I *have* to make that ferry sailing.

Although I had managed the cycle well yesterday I seem to be affected by a rather negative mood this morning. Yesterday I had felt a bit tired on the last seven miles but the thought of covering those same miles today, in reverse, fills me with less enthusiasm than I had yesterday. I buck myself up. I am fresh, it is perfect cycling weather and the light breeze is still issuing from the south which will help rather than hinder my progress. It is easy – but then again – perhaps I should get the 09.30 ferry instead?

Breakfast is a hoot. Normally hotel or guest-house dining rooms at 08.30 are decked with islands of tables, each holding the occupants of one room, who quietly munch their cornflakes, sip their grapefruit juice and agonise over how they would like their egg cooked. Conversation between guests is limited to "good morning!" or "could you pass the milk please?" There is none of *this* in our dining room. One big oval table holds six of us, the contents of five bedrooms (as far as I can tell). The result is startling. We have all introduced ourselves before the first rack of toast has arrived and by the time I am onto my second cup of tea we are on first name terms. Sitting so intimately around the one table has forced out conversation and shyness has consequently melted away like the butter on my toast. Breakfast lasts over half an hour – it is a tea party that we are having.

There is a chap who works for CalMac, a BBC researcher who has been eyeing up Gigha for a documentary and a lady whose family has taken their yacht up to Mull but have no room for her onboard. Lastly, there is the couple from near Campbeltown who boast that their village is in the record books for being the mainland village furthest from a

34

railway station, ninety miles in fact. "Give Railtrack a few more years and the record will be smashed," I remark.

I finally drag myself away from the breakfast table and load up the bike for the brief sojourn to the north of the island with all my bits and pieces, including my dry smalls. I am now back to the full quota of clothes needed for the remainder of the trip. As I leave, the BBC researcher is asking if she needs permission to climb the highest hill on the island.

The road north is a very pleasant country lane which winds its way past the small golf course and through various farms. I stop a few metres beyond Tarbert Farm to pat a friendly looking horse. My cautious feelings about my mainland cycle prevent me from carrying on to the very tip of Gigha. I have seen a fair bit of the island, however, during my stay. Far out to the north-west I can see the rolling mounds of Islay and the unmistakable profile of the Paps of Jura. Those islands are beckoning and in a few hours I will be there, hopefully. I turn my wheels around, back towards Ardminish.

I stock up on goodies at the village store where Mrs McSporran has donned her shopkeeper's hat. The usual fresh orange juice is purchased, a few rolls and I look for bananas. The carbohydrate content of these will keep me in good form, I reckon. I've always felt that eating a banana is like an injection of energy when out on the road. Trying to inject a banana is rather difficult, nevertheless. The only problem with bananas is that they do not travel well. This is not a problem today as the shop doesn't have any. An orange takes its place in my bag.

I bid farewell to Gigha at 10.30 and sail back across to Tayinloan on the *Loch Ranza*. When I step ashore on the mainland I have two hours exactly to cover the fourteen miles to Kennacraig. Lots of time – but I do not hang about. I still have my negative thoughts.

The bike is now wind assisted, as I expected it would be, and that makes a huge difference. I cover the first four miles in just over fifteen minutes and am consequently now a lot happier. The scheduled stop at Clachan for the orange is abandoned and I crank the bike into low gear for the climb uphill from Strathnafanary. Feelings are high – I will now reach Kennacraig with an hour to spare.

Crash Bang Judder! My front chainset seizes and I stutter alarmingly to a halt. I anxiously look down to assess the damage. The chain has come off the inner chain-ring and become wedged under a stud. Panic wells. For a few seconds I believe that my negative thoughts had been justified. Disaster has obviously been imminent. I should have taken the early ferry. I peer into my watch – I have eight miles still to go and an hour and a half left.

Out comes the tool kit for the first time and with a bit of fiddling with the screwdriver the chain is soon free. A couple of turns of the adjusting screw will ensure the problem will not recur. It only takes five minutes and I breathe a sigh of relief and unwittingly wipe my black oily hands down my brilliant white, freshly washed tee-shirt. Off I go again, content that my earlier worries had been justified and my troubles are now over.

My efforts going uphill are rewarded in the usual way with a terrific free-wheel down to the Kennacraig ferry terminal. There I can wash my hands, but not the tee-shirt.

The ferry terminal is cleverly disguised on a small islet linked to the eastern shores of West Loch Tarbert by a short causeway. The ferry is the *Isle of Arran* and she and I arrive on the pier at the same time. A considerable posse of cyclists is already there, waiting to board. The crossing will take two hours.

On most days in the summer there are three sailings daily to Islay, the ship sailing to the two Islay ports of Port Ellen and Port Askaig alternately. Today we are heading for the latter, where I have booked accommodation. The plan is to check into the hotel, dump my bags and skip onto yet another boat over to the island of Jura.

Islay is one of my favourite islands. From a distance it looks flattish and uninteresting, dominated by moor and peat bog. In fact it has a wide range of aspects, woodlands, lochs and beautiful beaches. I may have been very lucky but on all of my numerous visits to the island I have only experienced rain on a handful of days. It is a paradise for the birdwatcher and an oasis for the connoisseur of peaty, malt whisky. For the 'island-hopper' or touring cyclist Islay is an essential item on the itinerary.

The first time I visited Islay was in the summer of 1978 when I crossed to Port Ellen on that intrepid vessel *Pioneer*. Further holidays and visits have followed at regular intervals, sailing on such ships as *Claymore*, *Iona* and *Glen Sannox*. The *Isle of Arran*, recently deposed from the Brodick run by the larger *Caledonian Isles*, is barely eleven years old, the traffic to Arran has built up so quickly in recent years that she is now too small. Time will tell if she is the right size for Islay. She lies now, nose in, at the linkspan, her bow visor agape and her car deck looking like a huge empty warehouse awaiting the next load of vehicles.

The orange is consumed. I feel good now that I have arrived in plenty of time and 1 am looking forward to the sail and a good lunch. The remaining cycling today is likely to be a leisurely run across Jura to the village of Craighouse.

Choosing hilly and bleak Jura for my cycle instead of the flatter and more varied landscape of Islay may seem like a strange decision. The truth is that, as always, time is short and I have never cycled on Jura before. Craighouse seems like a nice easy target.

I cycled on Islay a year ago, having a weekend break on the island

36

with my three year old son Tony. He perched on a child seat at the back and both of us had a great time, me puffing up the hills and he entertaining himself for hours by poking his finger into the perfectly sized hole at the back of my saddle. My route on that occasion is worthy of mention as it is an excellent cycle route.

We started at Port Askaig which sits at the base of a wooded hill overlooking the mountainous Paps of Jura. Islay and Jura are separated at this point by less than a mile of violent tidal water – the Sound of Islay. Leaving the pier I pushed the bike and Tony up the steep hill to the lodge house above the hotel and turned left into the woods. From here a track can be followed through the deciduous woodland, past a couple of beautiful lochans, to emerge at the village of Ballygrant on the main Port Askaig–Bridgend road. Leaving the estate, just east of Ballygrant we took the small quiet road which heads south past Knocklearoch. The road took us across the hilly moors of the centre of the island and after a fair old puff we sped downhill to Cluanach before bearing right towards Bridgend. Islay has many such routes which makes it one of the best islands for cycling – provided the wind is blowing in a favourable direction.

Another passion of mine is birdwatching and Islay has to be the best island in the Inner Hebrides for birds. The huge winter flocks of White-fronted and Barnacle geese are well documented but the bird I sought long and hard on Islay was the chough. Several visits were spent scanning the cliffs and rocky coasts for this rare, large, red-billed crow to no avail. Then a local farmer pointed out to me that I was looking in the wrong places. Choughs prefer to nest in ruined farm buildings and feed on the grubs that inhabit the underside of cow-pats. What delightful fare. The secret to success in finding them is to look for a field of cattle near some deserted farm buildings. The area around Ardnave is a regular haunt. After his advice I saw dozens of them.

Another superb bird for which Islay is renowned is the hen harrier. This scarce bird of prey has never failed to show itself on my visits to the island – enough reminiscing.

The *Isle of Arran* loads a hefty load of cars, trailers, bikes and passengers. Finding space for everything on the car-deck seems like a work of art but I get the distinct impression the deck crew view the bicycles as an encumbrance. Various orders and arm-waving direct me to where I should place my machine on the deck. I do as I am told.

She sails on time at 13.00 and my thoughts return to culinary matters. What is on the menu today? Pasta? Yes, it has to be the lasagne and very satisfying it is too; served with broccoli. I am beginning to bore myself with nutritional statistics. How about a pint? No! It is too early in the day and I still have too many miles to go. I am beginning to argue with myself as well.

The weather is so lovely and the cafeteria so crowded that I take my lunch up onto the open deck. I feel relaxed now – another happy attack is on the way.

The ship sails down the peaceful waters of West Loch Tarbert and out westwards past the northern end of Gigha in a gentle curve into the Sound of Islay. From the shallow waters of the loch seals have emerged and are sun bathing on the rocks, taking little notice of the passing ship. After lunch I stretch out on the deck seats, doing a reasonable impression of a seal, and come very close to falling asleep. This is like a Mediterranean cruise.

As we pass the precariously positioned lighthouse at MacArthur's Head, which guards the entrance to the Sound of Islay, I take up position on the forward deck to watch our progress to Port Askaig.

The waters between Islay and Jura never seem to rest. The rushing tide creates eddies and a fierce current which today is rushing towards the ship. I can recall one occasion standing at Port Askaig watching a yacht, its sails limp, hurtling southwards at ten knots with the current, the helmsman clinging tightly to the rudder.

A small ferry, the *Sound of Gigha*, runs regularly from Port Askaig over to Feolin on Jura and is the sole ferry link to that island. I do not know the sailing times but I reckon it will leave Port Askaig shortly after the arrival of the *Isle of Arran*. In order to spend as much time as possible on Jura I want to be on that sailing. I do not want to carry my panniers around with me on Jura, however, so I plan to check into my hotel, dump my bags and rush onto the *Sound of Gigha* unburdened.

Our ship docks at 15.00 and I sit astride the bike on the car deck waiting to disembark with my heart thumping in anticipation of all the rushing around that lies ahead of me. The crewman grimaces at the accumulating cyclists and waves all the cars and trucks off first. By the time the last vehicle has rolled off the ship the car deck resembles the start of the Tour de France as around forty bikes of all shapes and sizes line up – raring to go. Meanwhile the *Sound of Gigha* lies waiting at her berth.At last the flag is up and away we go. I cannot help chuckling at the amusing spectacle.

All the other cyclists pedal a mere forty metres before pushing their machines up the steep hill out of Port Askaig. I don't have to cycle half that distance. I pull up at the hotel and unhitch the panniers as quickly as I can. I run inside to the reception. Still the Jura ferry sits at her berth.

Due to a minor misunderstanding my room is not ready but I dump my bags in it anyway."You're in a hurry to get that ferry, aren't you?" the lady of the house observes.I smile back, grab the back-pack, which I use for my bits and pieces when I do not have my panniers, and race outside.

The *Sound of Gigha* is still there, but not for long. We are off, yet again, to island number five.

On the way across a wee girl in one of the cars points to Ted, who is in his usual position at the back of the bike, and asks me why he is there. I give her a detailed account of his part in my journey. She seems to think it is a good idea to carry a mascot. Let's hope that he continues to give me good luck with the weather.

In my back-pack I carry the usual supplies that I have prepared or purchased in advance. Today it is a packet of CalMac smoked salmon sandwiches, fresh orange juice cartons, the essential midge cream, sun cream, camera and the ubiquitous OS map. Knowing that I am going to be pushed for time at Port Askaig I have bought my provisions on the ferry.

The *Sound of Gigha* leaves Islay at 15.30 and is due to leave the Jura side for the last time at 18.30. I have just under three hours and realise I can easily reach Craighouse, eight hilly miles away, spend some time there and cycle back to Feolin in time for the last ferry.

The day is pleasantly warm without being too hot and my legs feel very strong as I push off onto Jura. Cycling without the panniers will make a considerable difference to the effort required to get up the first hill. The road from Feolin passes along the raised beaches as it skirts around the southern end of the island. The landscape is wonderfully wild and unspoilt – all bracken and empty, pebbly bays scalloped out by the raised beaches, a product of the last ice-age.

Raised beaches are a prominent feature of the west coast of Scotland created by a process known as isostatic recovery when the ice melted and the land rose as the great weight of the frozen water oozed away. A bit like kicking your shoes off at the end of a busy day. The former sea cliffs then sit higher above the new sea level and a hundred metres or so inland. The Isle of Cumbrae has some good examples of raised beaches and also Jura where the entire west coast seems to be one long raised beach.

The *Isle of Arran* is making her way back down the Sound of Islay as I cycle parallel to her along the flat shore road. Then it is a stiff climb up over the moors, the single-track road turning eastwards. I stop regularly for a swig of orange juice and to let the occasional car past. I am loving every moment of the whole experience, free from the hustle and bustle, free from traffic, free from my panniers.

It takes just forty-three minutes to cover the eight miles to Craighouse which means I can allow myself an hour of relaxation there. The hotel garden is where I head for first and I allow myself the luxury of a glass of cold beer, to imbibe as I scribble my notes and swat the midges from my now blotchy, red legs.

I have always thought that the dreaded midge only makes his, or her, presence felt after rain or in the evening. I am painfully mistaken. The hazy heat deters them not one bit and I can count over fifty bites on each leg alone. Some people, I notice, seem immune to their bites, or perhaps never attract them in the first place. They have obviously taken a liking to me for some reason. Maybe all this orange juice that I am consuming is leaching out in my sweat and presenting them with a delicious cocktail. I later read that there are dozens of species of midge. When my trip is over I can verify that the Jura ones are the most vicious, positively Jurassic in fact.

Craighouse is a surprisingly verdant corner of Jura. The hotel and distillery dominate the village but several cottages and some shops are strung out along the narrow road which heads north to the quieter corners of the island. In the hotel garden palm trees flourish – the 'gulf stream' obviously heads in the direction of Jura after passing Gigha.

Beyond Craighouse settlements become rarer the farther north one travels. At Tarbert (another *Tarbert* – Scotland is full of them!) the island is almost split into two by a sea loch coming in from the west. A mile or two beyond Ardlussa the road becomes relegated to a track which continues to Barnhill where George Orwell wrote his novel *Nineteen Eighty Four*. The track continues to the northern end of Jura and between the northern-most point and the neighbouring island of Scarba lie the mile wide turbulent waters of the Gulf of Corryvreckan.

Corryvreckan is famous for its whirlpool. I have never seen it nor been to this very inaccessible part of the island – an ambition still to be fulfilled is to see the waters in full flood.

The whirlpool lies close to the Scarba shore and varies in intensity. Apparently it is created by the tidal waters escaping through the narrow channel between the two islands and being disturbed by pinnacles of rock on the sea bed. The power of the flood reaches a height when a spring flood tide travelling west meets a westerly wind. That must be worth seeing but as the northern tip of Jura lies some twenty-seven miles from Craighouse it is a sight that will have to wait for another occasion.

I could easily sit all day in the hotel garden at Craighouse. As I sip my beer I realise that I have only spoken to four people all day and three of them were in the catering business. My only *serious* conversation – not counting, "Can I have a lasagne, please?" was with the wee girl on the ferry over to Jura. Nevertheless, I do not feel so lonely. Who could feel sad or lonely on such a lovely day as this ? Now, the only chattering I can hear is from the families of swallows overhead.

My time is up. The last ferry back to Islay and my bed for the night leaves in one hour and I have eight miles to traverse. I have none of the anxiety that I experienced this morning about reaching *this* ferry.

The cycle back is great fun, it takes me only a little longer than on the way out and racing downhill to the shore the bike touches thirty-one miles per hour which seems fast enough on a gravel strewn road, especially as I have inadvertently left the cycle helmet at Port Askaig.

I sit on the shingle beach at Feolin waiting for the ferry to come over from Islay. Suddenly the sound of heavy breathing makes me lift my eyes and I am eyeballing a seal which has come to the surface just a few metres offshore. I consider having a conversation with him but he is gone before I can think of a suitable topic.

The ferry arrives and conveys me back to Port Askaig. I now consider myself to be "off duty". My day has been very successful, working out according to plan. Ten minutes after stepping off the Jura ferry I am in the bath.

Nobody seems to take a bath in a hotel, showers seem to be the norm. I lock myself away in the bathroom at the end of the landing and enjoy a wallow in a tub of water so deep that I am in danger of drowning and so hot that I quickly turn pink. Nobody disturbs me.

Later, as I prepare my belongings for the next day of travel, I glance out of my bedroom window and who should be pushing their way uphill but those other intrepid cyclists, Sandy and Kenneth. They had crossed to Islay on the sailing after mine, to Port Ellen, and will be staying the night at a guest house a mile or two up the hill at Kiells. We will all meet up again on the ship to Colonsay tomorrow morning. I look forward to a decent chat then.

My wife Clare, a mere thirty-five miles away as the crow flies, has a list of my hotels and guest houses and will telephone the appropriate one at nine o'clock each evening in order to check my progress. It is our only means of contact. This arrangement has been planned in advance and works well. By then I have been soaked, fed and watered, like a good horse and am ready for a chat – especially today. Tonight I have to take the call behind the bar, surrounded by bottles of some of the best malts in the land.

Still feeling fit at 21.15 I decide that I am obliged to do *some* cycling on Islay and so I make my way uphill, in the gathering gloom, to Ballygrant, in search of my fellow travellers. I search in vain but the barman in the Ballygrant Inn is in chatty mood as I quench my thirst before the breeze back down the hill to Port Askaig. I have carried my lights and heavy batteries around with me for three days now and at last this is an excuse to use them. The ride back to Port Askaig is gloomy and still and just a touch creepy. By the time I arrive back at my hotel it is dark and I am struck by that lonely feeling again. Best to get to bed.

Tomorrow I will be off once again on the *Isle of Arran* as she performs her once a week trip from Port Askaig to Oban, via Colonsay. I look forward to having some company on board but the longest, and as it turns out the hardest, cycle of the trip will await my arrival at Oban.

Day Three = 44 miles

Total for three days = 144 miles

41

Day 4 – Colonsay, Seil, Luing & Easdale

Wednesday morning and guess what – it looks as if another gorgeous day of unrelenting sunshine is beginning. I am no expert at interpreting weather conditions but looking at the totally azure sky it would be a pessimist that predicted rain today. And I am no pessimist. I don't want to take it all for granted, however. So I have adopted a "let's be grateful for what we've got" attitude to the weather. I am assuming each day that tomorrow it will be pouring with rain and this will be my last day of fun in the sun.

Breakfast has returned to the solitary affair at a little table in the corner of the dining-room but the view overlooking the Paps of Jura makes up for the lack of tableside chat. These mountains are also known as *The Maiden's Breasts*. She must have been some maiden – especially as there are three of them!

Outside after another bacon and eggs and half a gallon of tea. Cars and trucks are assembling in anticipation of the ship's arrival but I am in no rush. It is a lovely feeling not to be in a rush. My panniers are packed and loaded, my bill paid and I am out in the fresh morning air joining Sandy and Kenneth whom I locate in the middle of the haphazard queue of bicycles.

An attractive ketch, the *Leader* is occupying the only berth at the pier and has to move out to let the incoming *Isle of Arran* tie up.

The Wednesday schedule for the ship – sailing from Islay to Oban via Colonsay – is a very popular sail. Since the inauguration in 1989 of this route, Colonsay has become attainable as a destination for the day-tripper. Prior to this the three sailings per week from Oban meant that at least two overnight stays were required to visit the island. Nowadays, in the summer months a day visit to Colonsay is possible as the ship calls there on her way back to Islay in the afternoon. But it has to be a Wednesday!

Today, with the weather forecast excellent due to the persisting high pressure over Scotland, the day-trippers are out in considerable numbers with the prospect of a few glorious hours on the Isle of Colonsay.

The Wednesday roster must be a nightmare for the crew of the ship. At Port Askaig the vessel has cars remaining onboard for Colonsay and perhaps even one or two for Oban. They then have to load separately and facing different directions vehicles going from Islay to Colonsay and from Islay to Oban. At Colonsay they will have to load more cars for Oban and at Oban the whole process will have to be repeated in reverse. I pity anyone who has their car in the middle of the car deck, facing the wrong way and trying to get off at the wrong island. The crew know their job well, however, and we are all loaded onboard, bikes facing in the correct direction and sailing away from Port Askaig, just a few minutes late at 10.00.

The sail up the Sound of Islay always draws large crowds to the forward deck of the ship to watch the scenery and the birds that fly up and down the narrow channel between Islay and Jura, guillemots, kittiwakes, eiders, and, if you are lucky, a diver or two. We pass the distilleries at Bunnahabhain and Caol Ila on the left and the deserted raised beaches of Jura on the right. I am looking out for anything of ornithological interest while Sandy is scanning the waves for dolphins or porpoises.

Colonsay and her tidal neighbour Oronsay draw close. Unfortunately the ship will only tie up at Scalasaig pier for about fifteen minutes and thus preclude any cycling for me on Colonsay. I am sailing onwards to Oban before my next major cycling effort. I will have to get off the ship at Colonsay, however, in order to 'claim' island number six in my list of islands visited.

I have visited Colonsay on three previous occasions, arriving on *Glen Sannox*, *Claymore* and *Isle of Mull* respectively. It is a jewel of an island, possessing, in my opinion, the finest beach in the Inner Hebrides at Kiloran Bay: a mile of golden sands bounded by low rocky hills. With just the single hotel and with camping not allowed it is not an easy island to explore properly. Even the Wednesday day-trippers are required either to be at Kennacraig very early or to be sailing from Islay. Once ashore, especially with the weather as it is today, they will not be disappointed.

The north of the island has the best beaches and attractive, if somewhat overgrown, gardens and lochs around Colonsay House. The south has empty, rocky bays and low hills. Oronsay lies a mile off the southern end of Colonsay. At low tide the mile wide strip of exposed sand and mud can be easily crossed on foot. Visitors to Oronsay can reconnoitre the serene old priory in contentment and calmness, provided they have noted the time of the returning tide.

I am missing all of this today, sadly, but my strict itinerary does not allow me the luxury of a two day stay on the island – although one cannot find a nicer island on which to spend two days.

I skip off at Scalasaig pier and watch rather enviously as the dozen or so cyclists ride out from the stern of the ship and set off anti-clockwise around the island. Like Cumbrae, Colonsay has a circular road, which I once cycled around in the dark. Not to be recommended I can assure you; the imagination was running riot in the gloom.

The pier is bustling with folk coming, folk going and folk neither coming nor going. A passing lady, who looks as though she will not run away with my camera, is gently coerced into taking my photograph to prove that I have stepped ashore, albeit for the briefest of brief visits.

The *Isle of Arran* wastes no time and is soon on her way north again. Oban is over two hours away. I am, therefore, only two hours or so away from the main cycling adventure of the day, a good time to eat.

The food served aboard the *Isle of Arran* looks very appetising and the selection very varied – so I have lasagne again. I also stock up on provisions to avoid wasting time looking for them at Oban.

Unlike the other days of my journey I will be starting my cycle late. The ship is already behind time and unlikely to dock at Oban until 13.30. I plan to check into my bed-and-breakfast accommodation and jettison the panniers in order to cycle light yet again. I hope to be on the road before 14.00.

Sandy and Kenneth have also remained on the ship but have been invited to a barbecue at a friend's house near Oban. So it doesn't look as though they're going to do much cycling. Perhaps they're the clever ones.

My route will take me south of Oban, on the Lochgilphead road, in a quest for no less than three other islands. I spread out the OS map on a table and look at the route, paying particular attention to the gradients involved. Initially there is a steep climb out of the town, along the main road by the southern shores of Loch Feochan and then right at the junction with the B844. Uphill again and down to cross the famous 'Bridge over the Atlantic' to the island of Seil. From there I plan to visit the neighbouring islands of Luing, to the south, and Easdale, to the west. Both can be reached by small ferries from Seil but I have still to find out the times of their crossings and their frequency. I will then retrace my route back to Oban, having claimed three more islands and probably collapse in an exhausted heap.

It is going to be a hard cycle on a very hot day but I feel that the long sail is giving me a good rest. The prospect of such a cycle on roads and islands on which I have never been before is an exciting challenge.

The ship pushes onwards upon a deep blue calm sea. We pass the Garvellachs, an uninhabited archipelago of rocky isles. Onboard the ship an RSPB lady is assisting the keen observers in identifying the passing seabirds while being openly keen herself in securing their signatures on RSPB membership forms.

I get into conversation, on the forward deck, with a smartly dressed CalMac chap. Being fairly well rehearsed in shipping in the Western Isles I always have a topical list of sensible and informed questions in mind to ask these officials whenever I meet one. Like: why don't you give your ships more sensible names? Or, will you ever build more paddle-steamers? Or even, could you please put grilled sea-bass in a dill sauce onto the menus? He is polite with his answers (not to those questions of course) and seems interested in my trip. It transpires that the ferries of the Western Isles are having a very busy week.

We pass Insh Island, sailing between it and Easdale and Seil Islands. If only the ship could drop me off on one of them I would save a lot of cycling. We steam on.

In the Sound of Kerrera, on the final leg of our mini-voyage, the porpoises put in an appearance at last. Four of them dance in the bow wave of the ship to the delight of the sea-watchers and new RSPB members on the forward deck. Sandy is in his element. He's got a thing about fishy looking creatures, I am discovering, particularly when he's eating one.

Oban is a major culture shock to me. After days of peace and quiet I pedal off onto crammed streets full of noisy, fuming lorries and lanefuls of cars. I have never seen the town so busy and I have to keep my wits about me as I negotiate one-way streets and roundabouts on the way to my accommodation.

My room is rather dull but nevertheless comfortable. I stay long enough to dump my bags before setting off on the long cycle to my three new islands.

The road out of Oban is steep, dusty and hot. The traffic straining past me is disconcerting after having had so many miles of road to myself. I press on steadily, getting into my stride along the shores of Loch Feochan. A car creeps past me, slower than the others, and Sandy's bearded face leers out of the front passenger window at me.

"You're doing well, Stuart, I'm off to the pub!" He has succumbed to temptation, given the bike a rest and opted for an afternoon of trying to locate a 'real-ale' outlet with an Oban friend in a Volvo prior to lazing away the rest of the afternoon at his barbecue – lucky b . . . . The fleeting pang of envy briefly interrupts my flow but I power on into the breeze.

There are times on the bike when the legs feel very strong, energy is bursting out from the reserves and you feel that you can go on forever in a buzz of adrenaline. This afternoon I feel none of these. After turning off the main road and climbing the next vertical obstacle I am well and truly cycling into the wind and feeling tired. During the previous three days I have cycled one hundred and forty-four miles and fatigue is beginning to manifest itself.

The 'Bridge over the Atlantic' finally appears round a bend. The surprisingly high, arched stone bridge crosses a narrow channel of swirling water, like a flooded river, over to the Island of Seil. The bridge was completed in 1793 and is now a tourist attraction. I can see why. It is a bit of novelty crossing to an island by means of a bridge instead of a ferry. Whether linked by ferry or bridge, Seil is still an island and island number seven at that. The strategically placed inn on the other side of the crossing seems a good place to stop for a rest.

Seil measures about four miles by three and is new territory for me. I find it lush and prosperous looking – apparently the mother of the late Princess of Wales has a house here. By coincidence the Princess's mother-in-law had paid a Royal visit to Oban just the day before. If only she had lingered another twenty-four hours she could have cheered me on my way through the town.

My initial impression, as I head south through the island, is that Seil does not look like an island community. It has more of a rural village feel to it. I am sure that the easy link to the mainland has something to do with this. Would Skye start to look like this when the Skye Bridge opens in a few months time? I doubt it.

At the crossroads the way west leads to Easdale, I carry on south to Cuan, where the ferry to the island of Luing (pronounced *ling*) plies the narrow, turbulent Cuan Sound. I am not sure of the frequency of the ferry and so I press onwards as fast as the oncoming wind will allow. The road seems to undulate cruelly and I console myself that I should have a tail wind all the way back to Oban – provided the wind direction does not change.

At Cuan the council-run ferry *Belnahua* is moored at the jetty on the Seil side and I have a half-hour wait in the sun before it sails. I take a seat on the slate beach.

Cuan is a peaceful little community. Looking across to Luing there appears even less activity. The waters between the two islands are anything but peaceful. A dangerous looking current is carrying floating bemused gulls along at a fair rate of knots. One or two yachts creep tentatively through towards the sheltered moorings on the eastern side of Seil and Luing.

It is now 16.00 and I still have to get to Easdale. My soggy tomato sandwiches do not seem to be restoring the energy today, as they have done on previous days. My half-hour rest will be a help to me but I decide not to linger on Luing, and I'll definitely take it easy on Easdale. Despite there being several places of interest dotted around the island, time and tiredness are stacking their cards against me and I decide to spend only thirty minutes on Luing.

The *Belnahua*, named after yet another slate-producing island to the west of Seil, rumbles over to the other side with me, two other passengers and the bike, which is carried free of charge. I cycle a half mile uphill to a viewpoint looking eastwards over the island of Torsa. Torsa lies very close to Luing and I had considered paddling across the beach in order to claim yet another island. But the tide is high at the moment and I am not even sure if the island can be reached without a boat – or at the very least big wellies. I content myself with just savouring the view and the experience of just being here.

When planning my trip I had spent a lot of time poring over OS maps and, having never been here before, had only a mind's eye impression of these islands. Of course, the view is completely different from what I had imagined – but just as lovely.

Beyond Torsa another island is visible – the wooded Shuna. I cannot get there either. There is no cause for complaint. Luing is island number eight and island number nine is not far away.

Luing is a narrow, six-mile strip which, apart from being well known as a slate-producing island until the 1960s, is also famous for its red beef cattle. I regretted not being able to see much of it. That is the story of most of the visits to the islands, but then, I have fifteen of them to get to in one week.

Back at the Cuan Sound, sitting on yet another slate beach, waiting for the ferry to return for me, and it strikes me that all is not well. Perhaps the heat is getting to me but I am beginning to feel rather weak in the legs and just a touch nauseous. I take onboard some more orange juice in the hope that it will reverse the tiredness. It works for a while but I am puzzled because I have not really cycled many miles today.

Back on Seil I make my way to the crossroads and turn left towards Ellanbeich, where the ferry crosses to Easdale. I feel out on a limb now. Only my own efforts will get me back to Oban tonight. Twenty-odd miles of pedalling lie between me and my bed, but I still feel that I have to reach Easdale and not give up.

Another viewpoint – this time looking west to Ellanbeich and the island of Easdale a hundred yards or so offshore. I push on, down past the white-washed cottages to the jetty and the small motor-boat which is waiting.

I cross over to Easdale, leaving the bike and my bag on Seil. It must be the shortest sea-crossing that I have ever taken to an island. I am not unhappy at that as by now I am feeling quite queasy and light-headed. It is strange that when you feel below par physically your natural optimism and enthusiasm melts away. Everything is suddenly a threat or a potential problem. The boat is going to sink, the dog barking down at me from the jetty is actually rabid, I am not going to get back to Oban tonight but am going to die from exhaustion on this tiny little island. Negative thoughts are beginning to erode my morale and I am no longer the happy cyclist. I step off onto Easdale having already decided that this is also going to be a short visit. I go straight to the cafe for a cup of tea and a bun.

Easdale is tiny. Tinier than I had anticipated. It is a circle of rock barely half a mile in diameter, its centre rising to a rocky hill. The small groups of cottages are also white-washed and spaced neatly around the eastern side of the island. No roads, no cars and all beautifully peaceful. In the small harbour lies the unmistakable bulk of an old puffer, aground on the shore. The name of the cafe (*The Puffer Aground*) recalls its predicament.

Easdale is also famous for its slate. Much of the island had been quarried away before being subsequently flooded by the sea in a sudden storm. After that catastrophe the slate industry was finished on Easdale, although it continued for longer on Seil and until 1965 on Luing. A hundred years on, the landscape is still dominated by the quarries and the slate.

I am wishing that I had the energy to run up the hill, Dun Mor, for a panoramic view of the islands out to the west: the same islands that I had sailed past a few hours earlier. I sail back across to Seil, still clutching my polystyrene cup of tea to the bemusement of the ferryman. "Just a quick visit, then?" he jibes. "Are you island hopping?"

Unfortunately a lot of my visits are too quick but if I could afford to spend as much time as I wanted on the islands my journey would probably last a couple of months. Meanwhile my island hopping is over for the day and I am pleased that I have managed to achieve my goals. Oban now lies seventeen miles away and I am feeling rotten. How am I going to get there? At this point if Clare should miraculously appear with the car I would happily push the bike into one of the flooded quarries and take a lift. But she isn't sufficiently clairvoyant so there is nothing else for it but to push on as planned. Seventeen miles is not a huge distance in any case – it is just that pessimism is ruling the brain at this moment. I am rather disappointed in myself, my nutrition and my fluid intake have been more than adequate, I think. The sun is still beating down and its effects are probably taking their toll on me. It is 17.30, only seventeen miles, let's go!

Once on the road again I find that the prevailing wind is indeed now aiding my progress and I feel more encouraged. I stop at the inn beside the Bridge again and take on some more fluid. Once back on the mainland I only have twelve miles to go and the flowing adrenaline has improved my mood. My legs are tired but I now know that I am going to reach Oban fairly comfortably after all.

On the major hills I cheat – well, no-one is looking – and push the bike. I reach my accommodation at 19.30 and have a long soak in the bath. I am happy to be back.

Oban has a positively continental feel to it this evening – like Largs a few days before. The air is still warm and humid and the hazy sun seems to crawl lethargically over to the west.

The streets and promenade are crowded and the restaurants and pubs crammed with holidaymakers and tourists milking every drop of enjoyment from the unexpectedly warm weather. Everyone seems to be having fun but unfortunately I am not in the mood for joining in. I still feel nauseous and do not feel like eating – although I know that I should. I munch half-heartedly at a roll to try to restore my blood sugar but the only beneficiary is the seagull to whom I present the second half of it.

Left: Stuart at Lochgoilhead (1995) all loaded up and ready to go.

Below: The mirrored waters of Loch Eck.

Awaiting the arrival of the ferry at Dunoon Pier.

'Bute is Beautiful' Ettrick Bay.

The new distillery at Lochranza, Arran.

Sandy and Kenneth in the foreground at Lochranza as Loch Tarbert arrives.

Ferries signposted every way. I turn left, everyone else goes right.

Sandy aboard Isle of Arran
in the Sound of Islay.

That man again!
Sandy on motor boat
out to Mingulay.

The bike parked on the "Bridge over the Atlantic". Seil on the left, the mainland on the right. The Atlantic is underneath.

The grassy paths of Kerrera.

The Bridge linking Ulva (on the left) to Gometra.

On the Sleat peninsula, Skye.

Sandy admiring the 800 foot high cliffs on the west side of Mingulay.

The Trans-Uist highway, North Uist.

Beginning to feel the heat, Baleshare.

The crofts on Eigg.

Sandy off to investigate the Laird's House on Eigg.

Eventually I find a quiet corner in the lounge of one of the big hotels on the main street and sit down with a dram. The quiet corner turns out to be adjacent to the evening entertainment who suddenly appears and strikes up a noisy chord on his electric organ. I do not want to be serenaded and so move to an even quieter corner to write up the day's notes. As I sit down the singer starts his rendition of *Always Argyll*. After today I am glad to see the back of it.

Tomorrow is likely to be the easiest day of the trip with much less cycling. This will help me to restore my energy. All thoughts of quitting are now dispelled.

By now the hotel guests are clapping along to the music – time to go! I retire to my depressing little room and bumpy little bed and close my eyes hoping that they will not open again tonight and that tomorrow will come quickly.

Day Four = 38 miles

Total for four days = 182 miles

DAY 5 – LISMORE, KERRERA & MULL

YOU ARE NOT GOING TO BELIEVE THIS but the sun is shining again this morning. Am I really in Scotland ? The big orb is being very sporting in following the game plan with such enthusiasm.

A new day, new optimism and new islands await. I check out of my B n' B as fast as courtesy will allow and am down at the Oban railway pier with bike, panniers and Ted by 08.30. Today I am going to start with a visit to Lismore and being Thursday, the extra lunchtime ferry means I will have a couple of hours there before returning to Oban.

Kerrera is the target for the afternoon and although I have no timetable for its ferry I realise that I will have plenty of time to get over there and back, before my late afternoon crossing to Mull where my next B n' B is booked.

There are two ships at the pier. The *Eigg* is loading for the fifty minute crossing to Lismore and at the other end of the tourist budget the luxurious *Hebridean Princess* is taking on supplies for her next Western Isles adventure.

The *Princess* is the former CalMac car ferry *Columba* which plied these waters to Coll, Tiree and Colonsay before being superseded by the larger and more accommodating *Isle of Mull* in 1989. She is now a successful, if exclusive, cruise ship which undertakes week long cruises through the Hebrides giving a high standard of luxury to the forty-odd passengers hermetically sealed inside. On a recent family holiday on Iona we were greeted by appropriately clad American cruisers from the *Hebridean Princess* which was anchored out in the Sound. When they asked for directions I could not help asking if they were passengers from the ship.

"Oh yes – have you sailed on her?" one replied. Before I could respond, my wife Clare returned, "No, but he gets the brochure every year."

I join *my* little ship and am accompanied on the car-deck by a cement mixer. No luxury of cocktails here, unless I asked for one of cement and two of sand. At 08.45 we sail on a mill-pond sea across to the island of Lismore.

Lismore is one of the least visited islands on the tourist trail – undeservedly so. Back in Glasgow most folk have never heard of it let alone visited it. Now there lies a curious thing about Glaswegians (I should know, I am one). Much as they love Bute and Cumbrae they rarely venture up to the Western Isles. The islands of the Clyde are home-from-home but places like Mull, Tiree and Lismore are strictly for the tourists. It's not that Glaswegians dislike distant islands – they flock to Mallorca, Tenerife and Corfu every July – but the Western Isles of Scotland are deemed to be full of bogs, hills and midges and not a lot else, and of course there is nothing to do. *This* Glaswegian knows better, though they are correct about the midges!

I have stepped ashore once before, briefly, on Lismore but today I have the time and the means to explore a bit of it. It is a green, fertile island, sitting slap-bang in the middle of Loch Linnhe. Lismore in Gaelic means "great garden". To me it is island number ten on my quest to bag islands. I am not the first to be pleased to bag it. In the sixth century it was the scene of a race between two saints to claim possession. As they sped across on their respective craft St Moluag, realising he was going to come second best in the race, cut off one of his fingers and threw it ashore on the island to claim first landfall. I am in no such rush to be first off the ferry today, the cement mixer wins comfortably.

The craft that is carrying me, the *Eigg*, is one of six island class ferries run by CalMac.(The others are *Bruernish*, *Rhum*, *Coll*, *Canna* and *Raasay*). They all look the same, a bit like World War II landing craft, and do not need piers or even jetties to berth against. Like their D-Day counterparts they can run up onto a beach if necessary, although hopefully they will not be shot at.

I spend the time during the crossing poring over the prognostic OS map and thinking about how I am going to spend my two hours on the island. I said earlier that I am a bit of a OS map connoisseur. That is actually a bit of a euphemism. I'm obsessed with them. If the Ordnance Survey produced a 1:50000 series of China I would own some of them. As it is I have most of Scotland in the coveted purple covered series and once tried laying them out in order in my garden. I then realised I would have to climb up on the roof to make out the shape of Scotland. So what's the fascination ?

Well I cannot embark on any kind of cycle trip more than ten miles without one. Once you understand how to read them and comprehend all the little symbols and icons they allow you to visualise the lie of the land very easily. Routes and alternative routes can be planned and interesting roadside features, like churches with towers, windmills without sails and pubs, can be anticipated before you even set out. The only downside to all this is that for a trip such as mine you need several maps and they are very heavy. They are also expensive. If you live in Nottinghamshire, for example, you get your money's worth as the area is land-locked and there are no expanses of sea wasting space on the paper. But if you want to look at Tiree and Coll, for instance, you really are being fleeced because the total land area on the map occupies less than twenty percent of the space on the map. The price is the same, of course. Because of the route I am taking around all these islands I am effectively carrying around a lot of waste paper which will do no good at all unless I am caught short at the side of the road one day.

Basically I use the maps to predict climbs, find places of interest that I can visit and accurately measure the distances involved in each cycle. I like to know in advance if there is a three hundred metre climb around the next corner. It saves the feeling of despairing disappointment as you round the bend. I am glad, however, that I had cut down on the ten maps I had originally planned to take with me. My objective had been to post each map home after I had passed through the region that it covered, thus gradually reducing the weight of the panniers. I could post my dirty washing with them. However I find that I am not *that* organised, I do not have any large envelopes with me, and I end up carrying them all around the islands with me.

The map of Lismore suggests a rather bleak, moor-covered strip of land with one long road running up the centre of the island. The ferry slipway is half-way up the eastern side at Achnacroish. I decide, on studying the map, that I will cycle up to the northern end of the island – mainly due to the fact that the one and only cafe is at this end of Lismore and I am very partial to my favourite brew.

At the northern tip, where the island lies less than a mile from the eastern shore of Loch Linnhe at Appin, another small ferry connects. I plan to reach the northern tip if time allows. Just in case the cafe is closed I have brought with me my usual supply of bananas and orange juice. I had not brought bananas with me yesterday and am now blaming their absence on my energy crisis.

I pedal off at Achnacroish at 09.35 behind the belching cement mixer. It is a short distance uphill to the junction with the main arterial road. There I turn right and set off northwards.

I am immediately struck by Lismore's beauty. There is not much moorland and it is certainly not bleak. The road resembles the archetypal country lane, gently rising and falling and weaving between small lush fields, rocky outcrops and shrubbery. It is a very unspoilt scene, with real meadows of wild flowers and grasses. The island is certainly more varied and verdant than I had envisaged from the map.

I call in at the local shop where the owner bemoans the lack of visitors to Lismore. "The guide-books don't mention us", he laments. I assure him that I will sing the praises of Lismore to everyone I meet, and carry on northwards.

At the cafe a notice proclaims: "*CLOSED* – due to coffee morning at community hall". I have already passed the hall but decide to proceed onwards and call in for a coffee on my return. Opposite Appin I stop and sit upon a rock in one of those little meadows, munching the banana and watching a female hen harrier being set upon by a murmuration of mobbing starlings. It is 10.15, the sun is shining and I feel very good today. There is not another person in sight. I am completely alone. I suddenly have a little pang of guilt. What am I doing here at this early hour on a Thursday morning? Shouldn't I be at *work*? I am slipping dangerously into one of my happy moods and so decide to give myself a shake, stop raving and set off back down the country lane to find the coffee morning.

The community hall is conspicuous by the number of cars parked outside it – six! (Why hadn't I noticed it on the way up?) I park the bike, feeling quite confident that there is no need to lock it to a fence post and step inside – into a Women's Guild coffee morning in full swing. I pay my one pound entry fee and a further twenty pence to *name the dolly*. The "dolly" is a hand-knitted effigy and I name it after my daughter Philippa, because it vaguely looks like her – round-faced with a mop of red hair and a cheeky expression.

With my Lycra shorts and gaudy cycle top I fancy that I look like an alien amongst the silver- haired ladies who bustle about with huge tea-pots and tiered cake-stands full of home baking. I am certainly not treated like an alien but welcomed like a long lost friend. I am ushered to a table where I join Catherine and Roddy. Tea and delicious sand-wiches are showered upon us as we swap notes on our experiences of Lismore, hen harriers and coffee mornings. Catherine is on holiday on the island while Roddy rents a cottage on the island each summer. They ask about my trip and my route but as I chat I again experience that self-conscious notion that begs the question: what am I *doing* here, at a coffee morning on the island of Lismore ?

The hall is full of people, young and old, which suggests that half the island's population is present. I spot the island doctor and district nurse – obviously here in case someone chokes on a scone.

The wee lady with the enormous tea-pot comes around for the third time. She can hardly hold it up. "Tell me again, son, where have you cycled from?"

I down my third cup of tea and decide that I must have used up my credit by now. I cycle off back towards the ferry slipway having never enjoyed a coffee morning so much in my life, even though I fail to win the *name the dolly competition*. Who would have thought it would have a name like *Tabatha*? My all too brief two hours on Lismore will be remembered for tranquillity, scenery and hospitality. I do not spend a more enjoyable two hours during the course of my journey.

I cross to Oban on the *Eigg* in the company of a presumably empty cement mixer. It is after 12.30 when we arrive back on the mainland. *The Hebridean Princess* and a late running *Isle of Mull* are tied up. I hope to join the latter for either the 16.00 or the 18.00 sailing to Mull but between now and then I have another island to get to and no idea of when the ferry sails to it.

The answer lies two and a half miles south of Oban. The small motor boat which serves as the Kerrera ferry crosses from the mainland at the narrowest part of the Sound of Kerrera. I pause only briefly to buy sandwiches – there is not much to purchase on Kerrera – before making my way to the ferry point. I have a bit of a wait. The ferryman is across on Kerrera having his lunch so I sit out, in the now roasting sunshine, to have mine. The suntan cream, which has become a vital part of my travel kit, comes out again to be slapped liberally on neck and brow, although I have the feeling that it is already too late. I lock my bike to a signpost and remove my panniers with the idea of taking them over to the island and leaving them on the slipway while I explore on foot.

There are no roads on Kerrera, just a few miles of rough track. These are easily cyclable but I decide that for once the bike and I should part company while I go for a walk on the island. I leave Ted in charge.

Kerrera measures about four miles by two and lies less than half a mile from the mainland, separated from it by the Sound of Kerrera. Its northernmost spur protects Oban Bay from westerly winds and seas. On the OS map it looks about the same size, has the same angulation and is a very similar shape to Great Cumbrae on the Clyde. The terrain looks completely different; Kerrera is much wilder and rockier looking and, of course, lacks the circumferential road that everyone loves to cycle round. Looking over at it from the mainland the island looks very green despite having very limited woodland.

About forty people live on Kerrera – mostly sheep farmers – in a handful of dwellings linked by the rough tracks. I have never been on the island before, not for the want of trying, and am glad that I am having a rest from the heavy cycling routine. As I sit waiting on the ferry to cross I study my map, again! I decide that my walk will take me across the width of the island to the west coast. It is now almost 14.00 and I still hope to catch the 16.00 ferry to Mull. The walk, therefore, is going to be a fairly brisk one.

As I wait I get chatting to a Dutch lady who is going over to meet up with some of her family who are having a picnic. The trouble is that she does not know where on the island they will be! She has about eight square miles to chose from.

Ten minutes later I am on island number eleven and the panniers are dumped at the side of the track. The bike is, therefore, abandoned on one slipway and the bags on another. I am quite confident that both will still be there when I return. I set off up the track ahead of me while my fellow passenger chooses a southerly route.

Kerrera is not what I expected. It is green and lush, carpeted with grass and high bracken, with green pathways weaving in all directions. It is like a purpose built park designed for the rambler and walker. The feeling of total freedom and isolation is tangible. Although Lismore was also peaceful the two islands are completely different. You can *really* get lost on Kerrera. If I slip and twist an ankle here who knows when some-one will find me.

I set off across the grassy swaths and stony tracks towards the west-ern shore. A small sheep farm nestling in a wooded hollow is the scene of the only activity I witness on the island, two chaps are dipping their flock of reluctant bathers who emerge a strong amber colour. Perhaps I should dip my midge ridden legs in with the sheep.

On up the hill the heat is now more intense than anything I have experienced during this week of relentless sunshine. I spot the Dutch lady half a mile away on another track, scanning the island for her picnicking relatives.

I do not walk far on the western side of the hill. It is too hot and I choose to sit out the rest of my time, taking in the tranquil scenery. The sea to the west, stretching across to my next island, Mull, is almost unbelievably calm. I could sit here all day. What a wonderful way to spend an afternoon but if I want to catch that Mull sailing I cannot afford to sit around for too long and so after about half an hour I start retracing my steps. I now have to sit on the island slipway waiting for the ferryman to return. His boat is on the Oban side but there is no sign of the man himself. To cool off I dangle my feet in the sea but keep having to shuffle up the concrete slip as the tide creeps in.

The sun-tanned picnickers appear and ask the handful of people around me if anyone has seen a single lady anywhere. It appears that I am the last to see her so I secretly hope that nothing has befallen her as I will be certain to be the number one suspect !

I am just beginning to glance more frequently at my watch with my mind on my next ferry crossing when a car speeds up to the mainland slipway and the ferryman races down to his boat. When he reaches the dozen or so waiting on our side (where did they all come from?) he is very apologetic. "I'm sorry, I had to go to the bank and there was a queue."

We buzz back across on the powerful little boat and I am reunited with Ted and the bike.

I have half an hour before my ship sails to Mull and I decide to spend it on Oban pier. CalMac's intrepid *Lord of the Isles* is berthed and who should be lurking on her deck but Sandy. He and Kenneth have decided to head for South Uist and as the ship casts off we shout our respective itineraries (and a few mild insults) to each other across the widening gap.

"Did you get to Easdale?" he yells.

"Half of me did," I return. "Did you find some 'real ale'?"

"Too right I did," he shouts back.

It transpires that we will all be reunited on the same ship in two days' time at Tobermory. What intricate patterns we are weaving across the Hebridean seas. Perhaps their more haphazard way of doing it is the better way – they seem to be having no problem getting accommodation.

"Good," I think, "I'll have someone to talk to on Saturday."

The *Isle of Mull* arrives shortly after, running slightly late. Before I cycle up the ramp I catch sight of a fish van bringing produce to the *Hebridean Princess* which is still loading further up the pier. On the back window of the van it proclaims – *Turbot Powered*.

The ship sails at 16.10 and I descend to the restaurant, to seek shade rather than nutrition. The tea and the bun pass the time, however. I have sailed to Mull on many occasions – the first of which was in 1976 aboard the *Caledonia*, that dreadful ship which resembled the Leaning Tower of Pisa everytime it turned a corner. On a camping holiday three friends and I had intended walking around the island but the scorching heatwave of that summer put paid to that idea and we used the local buses instead. Apart from sailings on the *Isle of Mull* I have also crossed to the island upon the *Claymore* and, unusually, on the *Suilven*, when the latter made her one and only departure from her normal Ullapool/ Stornoway route in October 1989.

The *Isle of Mull* is ideally suited for carrying the many hundreds of day-trippers who cross to the island in the summer months, many of whom continue onwards across Mull on their pilgrimage to Iona. The 10.00 sailing from Oban and the 17.00 return sailing from Craignure, on Mull, are busy times for the ship's crew as these sailings connect with the Mull bus service which traverses to Fionnaphort and the ferries to Iona and Staffa. Both islands are definitely worth a visit – but beware those times!

Iona is, of course, famous for its abbey, founded by Saint Columba during his thirty-four years on the island (from AD 563–597). Over the centuries this important shrine to early Christianity has been rebuilt and restored and today it still retains a strikingly serene and ethereal atmosphere. It is a pity that so many of the tourists stop at the abbey and go no further as the beaches and bays on the west coast of Iona are exceedingly beautiful. I would have liked to have included Iona in my list of islands but my carefully chosen itinerary makes a visit impossible in the time available.

Staffa is famous for Fingal's Cave on its southern shore. Boat trips from Iona and Ulva Ferry on Mull convey those tourists with sea-legs, and some without, to visit the columnar basalt pillars, which constitute a large part of Staffa, and the famous cave, which is of cathedral proportions.

Sail out to Staffa on one of the sturdy launches that make the trip daily and Felix Mendelsohnn's *Die Hebriden* will be heard issuing from loudspeakers in a kind of aural assault which makes the gulls and guille-mots stare in astonishment and would have had poor Felix turning in his grave.

There is a third island nearby which I visited a few months before my trip and which has also become famous due to the pen of one of Staffa's previous tourists. It is the island of Erraid, a tidal island about one mile square which was the scene of David Balfour's shipwreck in R.L.Stevenson's *Kidnapped*. The sight of the golden sandy bays which link Erraid with Mull are worth the wet shoes that are inevitable on the stroll across at low tide. Stevenson visited Staffa in 1870.

Those are three islands which I do not have time to fit into my hectic schedule but are worthy of a mention. My target is Mull – but more of that later.

As we approach Craignure pier at 17.00 I am able to witness at first hand the returning exodus from Iona, Staffa and Mull. What initially looks like cattle-pens filled with stock, materialises into a human flock of several hundred sun-baked and foot-weary souls queuing for their passage back to Oban. I am rather glad to be heading in the opposite direction.

This time I am the only cyclist pedalling off from the car-deck. The other bikes have obviously been and gone. I am quite happy to be alone – after all I have been alone for most of the day, why should this leg of my journey be any different.

My accommodation for the night is at the village of Salen, eleven miles up the main road which continues to the island capital of Tobermory. It is still a very warm day but any worries that the fatigue and weariness of yesterday will be repeated are assuaged by the tail wind that I can feel on my back helping to push me on my way. I have a great cycle to Salen, averaging 13.8 miles per hour, fully loaded with the panniers and Ted, of course.

In my hotel room, freshly showered and with my feet hanging out of the open window, I am feeling a bit tired but very pleased with myself. The tiredness is more to do with the blazing sunshine and temperatures in the eighties than the cycling. I have, again, attained my target islands and it has been a most interesting and peaceful day. I am now on one of the most interesting and beautiful islands of them all.

I ponder over the choice of routes that I have for the following day over a pint and a pizza in the hotel lounge. In the morning I will head out westwards to Ulva Ferry and *either* sail over to the island of Ulva and hopefully cross its length to reach the neighbouring island of Gometra or else I can take the tourist route to Staffa and the Treshnish Isles. A sail out to the remote Treshnish Isle of Lunga to see the puffins is tempting but I decide to defer the final decision until the morning. Irrespective of the route chosen I will have a long, hilly cycle at the end of it in order to get to Tobermory where the accommodation for the last night of my trip is booked.

After supper I take a ride down to Salen pier where many a MacBrayne's steamer called. There I get quite a shock. The pier is in a dreadful state of disrepair, as is the ship that is moored there – the

Amaryllis. Debris is strewn all over the rotten and holed planks. The only signs of life are a pair of rock pipits which have built their nest in the ship. And then I almost get arrested! A police van pulls up and an officer of the law hails me, advising me clearly that I should get off the pier! I obey without hesitation.

It is now well after 20.00 and the sun is still surprisingly warm. The midges are becoming increasingly active and so I cycle back to the hotel to await my nine o'clock phone call from Clare. As I step off the bike the odometer trips two hundred miles, the distance I have cycled from the start of my week.

Day Five = 28 miles

Total for five days = 200 miles

Day 6 – Mull, Ulva & Gometra

IT IS GETTING DECIDEDLY TEDIOUS STARTING each chapter with the same sentence but for the sixth day in succession I wake to sparkling sunshine; the weather forecast each morning is getting boring. But I couldn't care less – the more sun the better as far as I'm concerned. I trained for this trip in howling gales and monsoon rains because I thought it likely that I would have to endure these kind of conditions in the Hebrides. But this constant sunshine is not typical Scottish weather. My fleece has remained in the depths of the panniers all week and I don't even know where my waterproof top is – I've not seen it since I packed it last Saturday.

It is only when I step outside before breakfast that I discover I am being smug, for there is a stiff breeze blowing up from the south-east. Over yet another breakfast of bacon and eggs, sausages, tomatoes, toast and tea I make my final decision on my route for the day. The voyage to Staffa and Lunga will have to wait for another occasion. A couple of factors dissuade me from taking this option. The wind might make a landing on these islands impossible thus rendering my efforts to reach another island void. The whole day could be wasted. The boat returning from the islands will not reach Ulva Ferry until 17.30 – leaving the start of the heavy cycle to Tobermory to rather late in the day. I will go for plan B. I will cross to Ulva and make my way across it if I can to the neighbouring island of Gometra, to which it is linked by a bridge.

Mull is a very large island, the third largest of the Hebrides, beaten only by Lewis and Skye. Looking at the map its shape has always reminded me of a profile of the puppet Punch. Where I am standing now would be his beady, malicious eye.

Getting around the far flung fascinating corners of the island by car involves a lot of miles and a lot of patience on the predominantly single-track roads. From Fionnaphort in the south-west corner to Tobermory in the north-east involves a journey of fifty-seven miles. Travelling by bike, however, is a cycling joy. The relatively quiet roads, spectacular coastal scenery and varied landscape of Mull makes it, for me, the hands-down winner of the best-cycling-island award. Tourists flock to Skye, and although the Cuillins and the Quirang are undoubtedly stunning the coastal scenery of Mull is in my opinion the best of any Hebridean island.

For the intrepid cyclist there are several on-road circular routes –

one of which I am going to follow today. For off-road mountain-biking there are many forest tracks and inland routes. Describing them here is outwith my remit and experience. My advice to anyone planning a cycle trip on Mull is to buy the three OS maps covering the island.

My route today will take me ten miles due west from Salen to Ulva Ferry on the west coast. After my proposed visit to the islands of Ulva and Gometra I will carry on clockwise along the coastal road to Achleck where I plan to take the unclassified road up over the hills and down to Dervaig. From this picturesque village, famous for its little theatre, the road winds and climbs up two more hillsides before dropping down into Tobermory. I will have to do this fully loaded but it promises to be an exciting day. I had considered sending my panniers on ahead to my hotel but couldn't persuade anyone to take them. Buses are infrequent on Mull and taxis expensive. They will just have to come with me. I also need to take some food with me and to this end the hotel supplies me with several doorsteps of lightly peppered tomato sandwiches. My lunches are as predictable as the weather – but much more moist.

I am quietly enjoying this hotel life. A hot shower and a cool drink. Something light to eat then a stroll around until nine o' clock when Clare phones me (the timing of her calls has been perfect). Perhaps another cool drink (actually there is no *perhaps* about it) then a good night's sleep. A hearty breakfast, a good scratch of the midge bites and then into the ritual of loading up the bike.

I especially enjoy this ritual. First the rear panniers go on with the things that I will require during the course of the day packed near the top. The appropriate maps will be slotted into the appropriate flaps. Next the bum-bag is arranged around the seat-post with valuables zipped inside and Ted peering out of the pocket. Tyres are checked, the bottle loaded with orange juice and the computer set to zero for the start of another day of statistics. I usually wear the helmet, especially if the journey involves a steep descent or traffic. During the hottest part of the day, and there have been many of them, the helmet can become uncomfortable and often ends up fastened to one of the panniers.

This morning I set off at 09.00 along the B road across the isthmus that links the east with the west of Mull. The strong breeze initially hits me head on. I smugly speed past an elderly chap on an old touring bike – only to be overtaken by him on the first incline; well, I am fully laden, with panniers and bacon and eggs, and not yet warmed up!

Turning right at Gruline the road continues along the northern shore of the stunningly wild Loch na Keal. I cannot stop staring out across at the scenery but try to keep one eye occasionally on the road in case I end up *in* the scenery. The morning sun is sparkling on the white wave tops that are being whipped up by the strengthening wind. The islands of Eorsa and Inch Kenneth guard the entrance to the loch and way beyond the seas around Staffa look sufficiently belligerent for me to feel that I was right to abandon the boat trip out there.

There are one or two climbs but I am now warmed up and they present no problems. Ulva comes into view as the elevated road around the loch turns to the north-west. A swift descent brings me to Ulva Ferry, which as its name suggests, is the ferry point on the Mull side which directly overlooks the island of Ulva a few hundred metres offshore. I have cycled ten miles and it is not yet 10.00.

Quite a crowd is gathered on the slipway – awaiting the boat trip to Staffa and the Treshnish Isles. Judging by the registration plates of the cars in the car park most of them are from continental Europe. As the wind whistles up the Sound of Ulva I am glad that I am not joining them and that my boat trip is only across a couple of hundred metres of water. Donald, the ferryman, helps me to load the bike into his small metal-hulled boat and gestures over to the crowd waiting on the slipway, "Strong south-easterly – they don't know what they're in for!"

By 10.00 I am standing on Ulva – island number thirteen. Its name means Wolf Island, but I believe the wolves are long since gone, at least I hope they are. Ulva is no more than an extension of the volcanic *trap* landscape of Mull. It measures about five miles by two miles lying east to west. Like Kerrera there are no roads but there the similarity ends. Apart from the mature deciduous woodland at the far eastern end, overlooking Mull, it is covered by very rough pasture and bare rocky outcrops which are home to several species of birds of prey. It is an island worth visiting, even if the traveller goes no further than the Boathouse Cafe and local museum, both of which are housed above the jetty. What Ulva lacks in roads it makes up for in well sign-posted tracks that reach out across the island to the many sites of natural and historical interest, such as the ruined settlements on the southern part of the island.

In the Boathouse, where I am depositing my panniers again, an Australian couple are setting off to find the homestead of their ancestral family. I hope they are on the right island – it's a long way to come to be disappointed.

I am setting off alone along the northern-most and longest track which spans the island to reach the neighbouring island Gometra, to which it is connected by a small bridge. The terrain seems rough and undulating on the map but Donald assures me that it can definitely be crossed with a mountain bike. He tells me this with such a heartening grin that it leaves me in doubt as to whether or not he is serious.

I set off at 10.20 and have only gone a hundred metres when I feel like turning back. The track is stony and rutted and in places frankly uncyclable. I persevere and push the bike. Past the farm, with cows looking at me in disbelief, and uphill through the woods. On clearing the trees at the top of the hill the track improves and for the bulk of the six mile trek to the Gometra bridge I am able to cycle rather than push.

The countryside around me is wild and empty, wilder and emptier than anything I have encountered so far. It really is tough going on the stony ground but I am in no rush and make slow but steady progress. My only concern is that I might suffer a puncture - the tyres are pinging off stones in various directions with alarming frequency and hideous noises.

The track winds around the hills on the north side of the island, neither losing nor gaining much height, merely undulating gently. By now the scenery is stunning, completely empty of people or cars or *any* sign of habitation. As in all the other days the sun is beating fiercely down upon me. The consistency of the hot weather is remarkable – Scotland is having its best summer in decades and the orange juice is disappearing fast.

It takes me an hour to cover the six miles and reach the far end of Ulva. I lay down the bike and produce the 'doorsteps' as part of a well deserved lunch. Down below me twenty metres away lies the little wooden bridge which crosses a narrow tidal stream to island number fourteen – Gometra.

The two islands are separated by a tidal gully fed by the seas to the north and south of the islands. The rickety, single-track bridge makes a humble link between the two islands. I have visualised this scene many times from the OS maps and it is rather a strange feeling to be now sitting overlooking this empty and rather desolate spot. I look around for someone that I can yell to: "Look, I'm *here!*" But there is no-one to be seen. It is another golden moment of my journey that I have to share with myself – but I am getting used to that.

Gometra is a circular, rocky island about two miles in diameter. Like Ulva it is privately owned and although the stony track continues round to Gometra House the owner prefers that bicycles are left on Ulva – fair enough. The once dilapidated house has been refurbished by the current owner of the island who has also purchased some Highland cattle to give it an authentic air. I would love to travel on but I have the return journey to consider and, of course, the cycle trip from Mull over the hills to Tobermory. The bike gets left on the bridge and I stroll over to Gometra. Like Seil two days ago, a new island reached by bridge instead of boat. I do not stay long – perhaps half an hour – and then set off back the way I have come.

I pause frequently on my way back across Ulva for a drink and, occasionally, to push the bike over the rougher parts of the track. About two hours after leaving the Boathouse I meet my first human – another mountain-biker coming towards me. We stop briefly to swap notes. He is also heading for Gometra, the island is enjoying two visitors today.

I am back at the Boathouse, overlooking Mull, at 13.00 having successfully completed what to me was an adventure. None of the civilised conveniences of Bute, Arran or Seil here! Had I encountered this type of wild terrain on the first couple of days of my journey I would have been terrified of having a puncture and being stranded. But by now, six days into my travels, I am a well-seasoned adventurer – or perhaps time and the two hundred odd miles have diluted my anxiety and boosted my confidence. I am hoping that my optimism will ride with me when I cross Mull this afternoon.

I find, as you will have noticed, that cycling alone makes me very introspective. Every now and then I pause to consider my well-being. How am I today ? Am I in fine fettle ? A bit more tired than yesterday, perhaps? Am I going to have a coronary going up this next hill ? Is that slightly light-headed feeling the first signs of sunstroke of the Kalahari Desert variety? When all my midge bites join up will my legs fall off? It sounds a bit mad. If I had a cycling partner I would be too engrossed in conversation to concern myself about my well-being, wouldn't I?

I have shied away from making these accounts of my journey sound like a cycling guide book, which I am certainly not qualified to write but I feel that the route across Ulva is worth summarising. A mountain bike is essential and suspension forks would be helpful if not compulsory (I did not have that luxury). A packed lunch is a must and plenty of time should be allowed for the route that I took. One further piece of advice: do not be put off by the first mile! The wild landscape makes the effort worthwhile.

Back in the Boathouse the charismatic Chrissie is toiling behind the counter, telling wonderful stories about Ulva and Gometra to her half dozen customers. I order a pot of tea and a small piece of coffee cake.

"I don't *do* small pieces," she retorts as she hacks a chunky eighth off the cake and presents me with it. When I tell her that I am cycling around the Western Isles and hoping to write about it she eyes me suspiciously. The BBC had filmed her preparing sea-food yesterday but I am hardly in the same league. After a couple of hours devoid of conversation her chat is a delight and the coffee cake delicious.

Sitting at the next table are a young German couple. I do not catch the girl's name but the blond haired chap is called Frank. I help plan the rest of their day for them with the aid of their map. They want to visit castles, so as Edinburgh is a bit far away I suggest Duart, and if they have time Torosay (both worth a visit – by the way). The rest of my day beckons. I cannot afford to sit sipping tea all afternoon, much as I am enjoying it. Donald has returned to the Ulva side and it is time to load up and go.

Moored at the jetty at Ulva Ferry, on the Mull side, is a motor-boat – belonging to the owner of Ulva. He has organised a fishing trip today but has miscalculated the tides. As he was loading his guests and their gear his boat grounded. The fishing party will have a two hour wait until some water returns. The poor chap is mortified. To make matters worse his craft fully occupies the stone jetty and Donald has to moor the ferry boat alongside, on the seaward side, and Ulva's tourists have to clamber over his decks to reach dry land. I give him a sympathetic smile as he magnanimously helps to carry my bike over. Things could have been worse – his predicament would have been the subject of a BBC film if it had happened yesterday.

At 13.45 with the wind now pushing me from behind I set off on the next exciting leg of my journey – to Tobermory. It is eighteen miles of smashing coastal scenery and steep climbs over the hills – the highest of which is one hundred and seventy metres. It is the last major cycle of my trip, once I reach Tobermory it will be effectively over except for the easy pedal around the island of Coll tomorrow.

The sun is shining down as ever but the air has cooled slightly from the effects of the SE wind. I feel great. So great, in fact, that out of my panniers for the first time comes my yellow cycling top. A quick change at the side of the road and off I go as if I were leading my own Tour de France – only at about a quarter of the speed.

The water-bottle has been replenished at the Boathouse and I still have some "doorsteps" left, although they are becoming soggier with every mile. My only concern is that the fatigue which hit me two days ago will return, as I am setting off at about the same time and in the same conditions. However, the distance today is only half that involved in getting to Seil, Luing and Easdale and I am confident that I will arrive in Tobermory in good fettle. In any case I have the faithful orange juice in the bottle.

The road running north and west from Ulva Ferry towards Calgary is a superb cycling experience which I would recommend to anyone who can pedal a bike (here I go with the cycling guide again!). The single-track coastal road climbs to around fifty metres at Ballygown but the ride high above the shores of Loch Tuath is so exhilarating that I hardly notice the weight of the panniers. The odd car passes me but while they have to wait in passing-places for oncoming traffic I can usually speed on and feel that over the distance I am travelling almost as fast as they are.

It is particularly pleasing to cycle a route that you know will only have to be crossed in one direction, especially if it is territory that you have never cycled before. I pedal onwards purposefully, gradually eating up the miles between Tobermory and myself. I feel that I am on a crusade. Nothing occupies my mind except the journey to the Mull capital. As each mile flashes out on my cycle computer I become more confident that this is going to be the best cycle of the entire trip. Tobermory will be sanctuary for me – my last major goal.

Just before the circular road climbs over the hill to Calgary I turn off onto the small unclassified road at Achleck. This is a short cut to Dervaig – but a hilly one. The road runs five miles to the village and I prepare mentally for the slog uphill at the beginning. At the road turn-off, however, I come to an abrupt halt.

A herd of about thirty Highland cattle is being encouraged from a field towards a new pasture somewhere up the road that I am proposing to go.

Nothing for it but to wait until the last stragglers go on their way before I can get on mine. One large bull with intimidating long, curved horns struts past me as I sit on the bike and then turns to look at me head-on from what I consider to be an alarmingly short distance. He has a belligerent look on his face and the farmer notices the anxious look on mine.

"Don't worry," he reassures me, "they're all docile."

I take him at his word and ring my bell to encourage my horned friend on his way. I chat to the farmer and help him to shepherd his herd up the hill. I ask him just how valuable these much photographed picture postcard beasts are. Anything from £4,000 to £20,000 I am informed. Pity I can't get one into my panniers.

The progress uphill is slow but I have plenty of time. So slow in fact that I never notice how much height I have gained.

I bid farewell to the chattiest farmer that I have yet encountered on my trip and goodbye to the *coos* as they turn into their new pasture. I am sure that there are no encounters like this on the Tour de France but I rather enjoyed the experience. I'll certainly never be frightened of a Highland cow, or bull, again.

I now have to pedal up the rest of the hill, stopping several times for a drink and to admire the view which is becoming more impressive with every metre climbed.

The woods and bracken verges have now given way to moorland. Soon I reach the summit and I am leaving the west coast of Mull behind. I glance back across the sea to the islands of Ulva and Gometra, some four miles away, and can just make out the bridge linking them. I appreciate, then, that I have travelled a considerable distance.

Ahead now lies the green valley with Dervaig nestling in it and the most exciting downhill ride of my journey. It is all I can do to stop myself laughing aloud as the bike speeds down the winding road, losing one hundred and seventy metres of height in just two miles. All the effort put into the climb is paid back with interest on that descent and I arrive breathless with exhilaration at Dervaig. There I sit outside the hotel with a large pot of tea to wash down the last soggy "doorstep" and to replenish any fluid that has been lost to the ever present sun.

Tobermory now lies only eight miles away along a tortuous road and over two hills. It is a slog and I admit to a bit of pushing. The road turns one way and then the other around a series of hairpins and I have the wind alternately aiding and then hindering me.

Another breeze downhill. I am just congratulating myself on my efforts when I spot the next climb ahead. The road looks as though it is snaking up a mountain but once into the climb it does not seem too bad: head down, gears low and keep pedalling. Much orange juice is consumed but I know that when I reach the top of this hill I am as good as at Tobermory. I take my time and when I reach the shores of Loch Carnain an Amais my head is buzzing – with orange juice, adrenaline or altitude sickness I do not know but I feel on top of the world. Tobermory is now just three miles away – downhill. Gravity does the rest.

The map comes out for the last time and overhead a series of deep "cronks" heralds the presence of a pair of ravens. The final descent is a corkscrew course through the picturesque streets of Tobermory and I finally come to a halt at the waterfront at 16.35. I feel like stopping everyone I meet to boast about the day's achievements.

"I've been to Ulva and Gometra, you know! I've climbed over the hills from Dervaig to get here. I've cycled forty miles and patted a *heilin coo*! I wasn't going to pat the bull now, was I?"

As usual I have no option but to keep all this to myself, but I am very chuffed. The toughest parts of my journey are all behind me now. I am tired and a touch light-headed but feel none of the nausea or weakness that I experienced two days ago. The legs still feel good, even if they don't look good, but my hands are sore from clutching the handlebars tightly on those descents.

I check into my hotel and tie the bike up for the night in the courtyard. It deserves as much of a rest as I do. Another pot of tea and a hot bath are next on the agenda.

Tobermory is rightfully described in the travel guides as one of the prettiest villages in Scotland. The buildings on its waterfront are painted in a rainbow of colours and the restaurants and gift shops reflect the affluence of some of its visitors – many of whom arrive by yacht. It is built around a wooded, sheltered bay beneath whose waters lie the remains of *Almirante de Florencia*, the doomed Spanish galleon which finally came to rest here in 1588 following the Armada rout. Did it carry gold?

Feeling refreshed I wander up to the pier. I will be leaving Mull from here early tomorrow morning on CalMac's *Lord of the Isles* but at the moment it is one of their smaller ferries *Coll* that is berthed, loading traffic for the crossing to Ardnamurchan. I decide to join it for the return crossing but when I climb onto the upper deck there is nowhere particularly inviting to sit and so I give it a miss and get off again. I complain to one of the crew. "There's no decent place to sit."

"Oh they had to change the seating," he explains apologetically, "you know the wooden seats that are supposed to float in an emergency?"

"Yes, I remember sitting on those."

"Well we tested them – and they sank. We had to get rid of them."

A sister ship of the *Coll*, the *Bruernish*, is bobbing about in the bay, tied up as spare vessel.

Quite unexpectedly, at 18.15 precisely, something very unusual happens – something that has not occurred at any time during the previous five days – it starts to rain. Big slops of rain are peppering my fish supper as I sit on a bench looking out at the bay with my feet up on a railing. The six days of heat and sunshine had not been expected but now that the bulk of my cycling is over I am caring less what the weather is offering now.

I feel as though I have been away from my home and my family for such a long time – Arran and Gigha seem weeks ago. I have less than twenty-four hours to go before being reunited with Clare and the children and I am rather looking forward to that.

I pick at my dampening haddock and chips. My eating habits are puzzling me. After a long day in the saddle I would have thought that I would be pushing my way to the head of the queue of the first eating place I encounter. Instead my appetite is minimal. I am empty rather than hungry but otherwise feel fine. I blame it all on my hormones and decide that there is nothing wrong with picking at my food.

My thoughts go from supper to breakfast as I can envisage a potential problem arising from my early start tomorrow morning - namely that I might not get any breakfast. My plan for the following morning is to sail from Tobermory at 07.45 to my last island, Coll. Such an early start poses a question mark over whether the hotel management will keep to the second part of our bed n' breakfast agreement. I might pick at my supper but breakfast is a different matter. I love my breakfast!

I need not worry. The hotel supplies me with a trayful of goodies for the following morning: fresh orange juice, grapefruit, bread rolls. I can hardly wait until morning. Before that, however, I decide that I have to visit that famous Tobermory watering-house – the Mishnish.

In what is always a hive of activity, particularly with foreign tourists and yachts-people, I pick the only quiet corner and to my surprise find myself sitting next to Frank, the German chap to whom I had spoken on Ulva.

We end up having a very pleasant evening to ourselves that must have gone a fair way towards improving Germanic-Scottish relations; all due to his excellent English rather than my non-existent German. I buy him a Bunnahabhain, he likes the malt in the "fat green bottle", and he buys me a Lagavulin as we swap travel stories. I learn from him that Bavarians are rather arrogant and he learns from me that it is not a good idea to park a hired car on the Royal Mile if he intends to enjoy his proposed visit to Edinburgh.

After six fairly solitary days it is a joy to have such a long conversation with someone. It seems appropriate that it should occur on my last night. Despite my protestations to the contrary he insists on buying me

Lagavulin number two. I eventually let him. More animated chat and then we shake hands with the liquor score remaining Germany two Scotland one.

In my very cosy hotel room I study the bedside magazine supplied for the guest's enjoyment before dropping off to sleep. An interesting article on Israeli–Egyptian relations seems historically familiar until I look at the front cover and find that the magazine dates from 1982.

I fall asleep looking forward to my breakfast – already half-eaten on the tray beside me.

Day Six = 40 miles

Total for six days = 240 miles

Day 7 – COLL

THE ALARM BUZZES AT 07.00 and I creep about quietly getting my panniers packed for the last time. A sharp pain draws my attention to my right forearm. I had been bitten there by a cleg yesterday – a present from one of my Highland cattle friends. I now have a nine inch long swelling extending over a large area of my arm but I am not particularly worried if I start to fall apart now – I have only one more island to go.

The *Lord of the Isles,* or *Lottie,* as she is affectionately known by steamer buffs, is the busiest of all CalMac vessels, serving the Inner Hebrides of Coll and Tiree and the Outer Isles of Barra and South Uist.

The previous evening she would have left Barra, with Sandy and Kenneth aboard, arrived at Oban at 05.00 this morning and turned around an hour later for her Coll and Tiree sailing. She should be half way up the Sound of Mull by now, with my two fellow travellers aboard. They were planning to stay on the ship at Oban when she returned from the Outer Isles. She will call in at Tobermory on both the outward and inward sailings. I will join her here at Tobermory and sail to Coll. I could stay aboard and pay very brief visits to both Coll and Tiree but would not have time to cycle on either so I have planned to spend a couple of hours on the former island rather than *bag* Tiree. I will then rejoin the ship on her inward sailing to Tobermory and hence to Oban. At Oban my journey will be over and my family will, hopefully, be there to meet me.

I join the small crowd on Tobermory pier and sit down on a bollard to scratch my midge bites and study the assortment of pale, tired faced tourists around me. One or two of them are framed by ridiculous hats, but then I probably look a pretty picture myself. I dig into my bags for the remains of my breakfast.

It is a dull morning but still mild and dry. The midges are out in force – do they ever sleep?

My mind goes back a few years to a similar trip when a friend and I had a bit of hanging about to do on Tobermory pier for the very same ship. We had sailed over to Craignure on the *Claymore* and caught the bus to Tobermory with the aim of sailing back to Oban upon the inward bound *Lord of the Isles.* On reaching Tobermory we discovered that *Lottie* was running late. We adjourned to the Mishnish but were concerned that we might miss the boat. The CalMac staff were very helpful, however and offered to come and drag us from the pub as soon as the ship arrived. An hour later they were true to their word as the pier-master poked his head around the door: "That's your ship coming now." That is what I call service. Today I take no chances – in any case the Mishnish is not open at 08.00. I relate the story, however, to the chap in charge in the CalMac office before rejoining the group of fellow travellers on the pier. A mere five minutes later the pier-master sticks his head out and announces, "The *Lord of the Isles* is running forty minutes late!" And then pointing over at me: "And it's all that man's fault."

Everyone glowers at me as I shrug helplessly. I think they believe him. *Lottie*'s late departure has cost me a hot breakfast, I now have time on my hands. The delay, I later learn, was due to her having to perform an extra run between Coll and Tiree yesterday to pick up traffic that had been booked for her but for whom she had no room on her scheduled sailing. A computer error no doubt.

By the time that *Lottie* turns round Calve Island and into the Bay it is 08.40 and the people in the funny hats have definitely ostracised me.

She ties up, lowers her starboard ramp and I pedal aboard. We sail exactly one hour late. Of my friends Sandy and Kenneth there is no sign – perhaps they have been stranded in South Uist and are not aboard at all. I retire to the restaurant for the hot breakfast that I had been denied.

We sail out of the Sound of Mull with the lighthouse at Rubha nan Gall on our port side. The lighthouse "garden" had been the scene of a camping holiday for me during the summer of 1976. That, for me, was the hottest and sunniest summer I had known – until this one!

On the first night of that holiday we experienced a thunderstorm which the tents survived fairly well. However, on awakening, we found not one but two dead sheep within a few metres of us. We never discovered what killed them but each time since that I have sailed by Rubha nan Gall and stared across the water at the lighthouse the sultry and foreboding atmosphere of that visit has been evoked in my mind. It is always the most fleeting, ephemeral of feelings but it takes me right back to the scene all those years ago and it is quite creepy. As I look across to the lighthouse now I get that sensation again.

As the weather is somewhat cooler I don the long cycle leggings for the first time on my trip in preparation for my circumnavigation of Coll.Strolling along the open deck I bump into a sleepy-looking Sandy. He has just emerged from his cabin in the bowels of the ship having stuck to his plan and sailed from Lochboisdale. He and Kenneth intend staying aboard to Tiree and thence back to Oban, thereby completing a mini-cruise of nineteen hours and six piers.

I study the OS map of Coll and finalise my route around the island. Coll is a thin and low-lying strip of land forming the less populous of the out-lying Hebridean pair of Coll and Tiree. Its micro-climate is one of above average sunshine, below average rain and much wind. There is one village, Arinagour, several crofts and small farms and many damp meadows that are home to that rare and secretive bird the corncrake. The presence of the latter has led the RSPB recently to purchase a fair chunk of the island as a means of protecting the fragile habitat of these once numerous birds. Perhaps their rasping calls will soon be heard more frequently.

From Arinagour the road leads north and south and forms a near circle. The loop is incomplete due to a mile and a half of sand-dunes on the western side of the island. According to the map a track crosses the dunes and by negotiating this I can complete my circle. I intend to try this in a clockwise direction but only have two hours in which to do so. My main concern is that the track across the dunes is impassable and that I will lose my bearings. The ship will call back into Arinagour at 12.30, assuming that she is still running late, and I have to be on her in order to get home today. I am also worried that *Lottie* might make up time on passage to Tiree and my time on Coll might be reduced so I will have to be back at Arinagour pier by the scheduled time. That will mean a fairly speedy cycle but one which I can do light, as I can leave my bags behind on the ship. Due to my exaggerated fears that something catastrophic is going to happen on my last island, based purely on the fact that *nothing* catastrophic has happened on any of the other islands, I decide to take the full tool kit with me.

Coll should be an easy island to finish with. In my two hours I am likely to see a fair bit of what it has to offer. I remember as a child writing an adventure story based on the island of Coll – an island plucked arbitrarily from a map of Scotland. In my mind's eye it was a hilly, densely-wooded island and I described it as such. Of course the truth could not be more different. In fact, on the approach from Tobermory the landscape of the north-eastern corner of the island appears distinctly lunar. The beaches and deserted bays look tempting however.

As on all the other days the weather remains dry throughout my visit – a quite remarkable feat considering the vagaries of Scottish weather. The sun is a touch more insipid today, but this makes a welcome break from the heat.

We arrive at Arinagour and the ship backs onto the new linkspan, still an hour late. I wave goodbye to my friends who remain aboard.

"Bye Stuart, make sure you are back on the pier in time," jeers Sandy. I watch the ship sail off southwards – not certain exactly when she will return.

Arinagour is an attractive village comprising church, school, post-office, hotel and a shop – which is closed. I always find it strange that in small communities such as this which depend on the ferry the village stores are shut when the ship arrives and the visitors come flooding ashore.

71

I head south, through a small wood and onto the bleak moorland road. I feel very fit today, perhaps because I know that this is the last island of my trip and an easy cycle. Due to my uncertain timetable I press on at a good pace.

My first stop is at Breachacha where I seek the graphically named Struthan nan Ceann which translates to "the stream of the heads". This tiny burn was the scene of a battle in 1593 between the clan McLean of Coll and the invading Duarts. Apparently the burn became filled with the severed heads of the invaders. From a hundred metres away, as I scan the fields, a red blob beside the burn has me worried but it turns out to be the post-box. The only thing floating in the burn today is a duck. As a non-speaker of Gaelic I often wonder what other historical wonders are locked up in the innumerable Gaelic placenames of the Highlands and Islands; the "valley of the lost cyclist", perhaps.

At the road junction I turn right, northwards, to continue my circle. I reach the end of the road and the beginning of the sandy track that crosses the dunes of land owned by the RSPB. I set off, hopeful that the road will re-emerge on the other side of the dunes, a mile and a half away, and that my route through the sand will coincide with it.

The tussocks of coarse grasses and sand make navigation difficult while the rough terrain, riddled with rabbit holes, makes it crucial that I keep my eyes down to check the progress of my front wheel.

This small part of Coll is dramatically barren and devoid of people, just the birds and hundreds of distinctly melanistic rabbits.

I am relieved to find that the track is fairly obvious, albeit tortuous. I bounce up and over the grassy banks fancying that from a distance I look like Steve McQueen, in his famous scene from *The Great Escape*.

I have an hour before I am due back at Arinagour but lay the bike down for a few minutes. I can hardly visit the west coast of Coll without seeing the sea. What better place to pick than Hogh Bay and its beautiful sands. Completely empty, the Atlantic breakers are roaring up the beach. The next land to the west is the American continent. Standing there, buffeted by the wind, I feel as though my nearest contact with civilisation is a million miles away. This induces in me a feeling of urgency and I am soon on my way again.

With relief I find the gate that marks the continuation of the circular road and, after pausing to look at the new community building, opened by Prince Charles only one month ago, I am off onto the tarmac once more.

The west coast of the island is noticeably rockier than the east but seems to have more sandy bays. The road twists more and the wind is often blowing in my face now. I meet another cyclist and we stop to chat. He is also attempting to circle the island, but anti-clockwise. He is, therefore, even more pushed for time than I am as he too is planning to catch the ferry at Arinagour but has further to go now than I have.

He decides to cycle with me back to the village. It transpires from our conversation that he is also on a cycle trip of his own design and we try to figure out where our paths may have crossed.

Past Arnabost we turn south on the last leg of the circle and into the teeth of a blustering wind. The last two miles are a hard pedal.

Arriving at the hotel I step inside for a well-deserved drink. I have completed the circle with time to spare – island number fifteen has been circumnavigated. All that is left now is to roll downhill to the pier. I have a wander around the hotel garden and then climb upon the bike for the last time.

On that last half mile I suddenly feel that I do not want to reach the end. After all those miles – more than two-hundred and fifty – the bike is now rolling downhill itself, and I am trying to stop it, or at least slow it down. It is all over bar the three hour sail to Oban. A few people are strolling down to the pier alongside me. I want to stop them and announce: "I've been on fifteen islands in a week, you know!"

I have completed my itinerary with great success and a with a great sense of personal fulfilment. Out to sea the *Lord of the Isles* is ploughing onwards on her return from Tiree. I park the bike and seek shelter from the strong wind behind a concrete wall on the new pier. There I scribble into my notebook for the last time.

The ship arrives, still running an hour late, ties up and Sandy and Kenneth are still aboard to wave to me as I cycle onto the car-deck. I had considered hiding on the pier until the last minute to shock them into thinking that I had been delayed and missed the boat. They, on their part, had with similar mischief thought about hiding my panniers, which I had left on board. As it turns out we all behave ourselves.

I am glad to get back aboard and warm up. It is the first time that I have felt cold in a week.

In the restaurant I tuck into mince and tatties and then keep my appointment with Sandy in the bar. Now that our respective trips are all but over we can relax, reminisce and swap nautical and cycling stories. Sandy's trip may have been spur of the moment but a fair bit of planning had gone into mine. The one thing that I could not have planned in advance was the weather. The constant sunshine helped to make the trip very enjoyable. There was another benefit, apart from my personal comfort. I was able to view each of the fifteen islands in the same light. They were all sunny and bright and I was able to compare the experiences of each day without being influenced by meteorological factors.

Looking back I have several particularly favourable moments and would not like to put one island above another in order of merit. All the islands provided some wonderful moments for me, with the exception perhaps of Easdale, for which Easdale is not to blame. I would have to admit that for the cyclist, Mull is hard to beat.

I loved my peaceful morning on Lismore, my afternoon heatwave on Kerrera and my soul-searching sunset on Gigha. To get an opportunity to sail and cycle around the islands of the west coast of Scotland was a wonderful privilege – an ambition of many years that I had at last managed to fulfil.

The ships had not let me down and neither had my trusty mountain-bike. I was quite happy with my own performance as well. Good preparation had accounted for the latter.

I had pedalled two hundred and fifty-five miles and sailed around one hundred and ninety nautical miles. I had sailed on fourteen vessels and taken one train.

Looking at a map of the west coast of Scotland my travels seem fairly awesome to me, considering that I had never made a journey like this before. Looking to the north and west, however, there are a lot more islands still to be cycled. There will have to be a part two to the story.

At 15.50 we turn into Oban Bay and there is one last delay. The Mull ferry *Isle of Mull* is ahead of us and takes precedence at the pier. We sit out in the bay until she leaves. Through a pair of borrowed binoculars I can see my family standing on the pier, waiting to greet me – my children wave frantically. I wave back.

Day Seven = 15 miles

Total for seven days = 255 miles

INTRODUCTION to the 1999 TRIP

IT TOOK FOUR MORE YEARS TO FIND a suitable time slot to add part two to my travels. It wasn't four years completely devoid of cycling in the Western Isles. I embarked on a few one day trips in amongst the islands and peninsulas of the Clyde in the interim. Notably a two-day cycle in August 1997 from Dunoon to Campbeltown, down the west side of Cowal and the east side of Kintyre using the Portavadie/Tarbert ferry and returning home via the paddle-steamer *Waverley*. In June 1996 Sandy and I took a memorable trip with our bikes from the northern tip of Jura to Port Ellen, using a speed-boat of all things to propel us across to Jura from Crinan.

When the time came to stitch more islands together and add them to the 1995 expedition I found Sandy very willing to participate. His son Kenneth was less enthusiastic and decided to stay at home this time. My only pre-condition was that I wanted to plan the route and itinerary. Sandy was happy with that.

Our route may seem unnecessarily complex but you have to remember that I am a steamer/ferry buff as well as a cyclist, which means I'm doubly mad and therefore take the most complicated route to get from one point to another. To simplify our route it can be broken-down into three parts; firstly a trip to Barra to visit a few of the islands at the southern end of the Western Isles archipelago, then a couple of days based at Mallaig to allow us to visit Eigg and the Sleat peninsula of Skye, and then a return to the Outer islands to cycle in a big arc up the Uists to Harris and back to the mainland via Skye. I reckoned we could get to about fifteen islands (as in 1995). Again I will let the route unfold as the week progresses.

By now I was an expert on what to pack in the panniers; much the same as last time actually. As for the fitness: I trained a bit harder. It is all very well when you travel alone and you start to feel tired halfway up a hill and you lie out for a quick snooze to recover, but this time I had company and I didn't want to embarrass myself by collapsing knackered in a heap while Sandy pedalled wistfully on. So I trained and moaned to him about how unfit I was. In fact he did the same and we had conversations on the phone like:

"I've not been for a cycle for weeks now . . ."

"That's nothing. I've forgotten what colour my bike is . . ."

Pathetic isn't it?

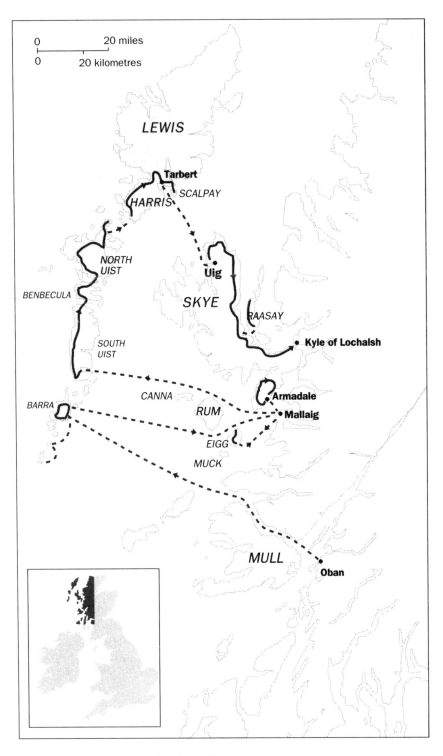

1999 Map of Second Journey
Start: Oban *Finish*: Kyle of Lochalsh

DAY 1 – BARRA & VATERSAY

RENDEZVOUS POINT IS OBAN RAILWAY PIER at 14.00 on Saturday 7 August 1999. Sandy is there, with his wife and mother-in-law to bid him farewell, or perhaps to make sure he goes! There is an air of excitement. Will all our ferry connections work out? How many islands will we get to? How many miles will we cycle? Will we still be speaking to each other at the end of it all?

Our personal commitment to our preparations for this trip have been remarkably thorough and reassuringly similar. I've been lounging about in Tuscany, eating loads of pasta and pizza and drinking too much Chianti and Sandy has spent the last three weeks in the United States where he has put on so much weight that he can barely fit into his new cycling jacket. Great! It augurs well for the next two hundred and fifty miles. Fortunately the cycling will actually start gradually and it will be the fifth day before we have any cycling over forty miles with our panniers. The first few days will consist of a boat trip or two and a few easy day-trips without our bags.

The ship taking us to our first island, Barra, is the fairly new *Clansman*. She has just taken over from the trusty *Lord of the Isles* as the Oban to Coll/Tiree and Oban to South Uist/Barra ship. I had already been aboard her once, from Ardrossan to Brodick when she relieved on the Arran service and already have mixed feelings about her. She is very comfortable, with an interesting layout but there is very little open deck space on top and there are no cabins for the weary Western Isles traveller coming home after a busy week at the office. Not that we have to worry about that, of course.

She arrives on time and we pedal aboard the car deck. At 14.50 precisely we're off – on part two of the adventure that we started independently of each other four years ago.

From the small rear deck we can wave to our families as the gap between us and the pier gets wider and I can no longer make out any of the children with any certainty (I only have the four, you understand). We remain outside to catch up on our news and to update our plans. At the outset we had the idea of having several meetings to carefully plan the finer details of our journey. But this concept had actually boiled down to one meeting in the pub and a couple of phone calls. Sandy trusted that I would turn up with a good route and I trusted that he would turn up.

Actually we had agreed a few sensible compromises on what we carried in our panniers. I agreed to carry the OS maps (seven maps adds up to a lot of weight) and the medical kit – I was hoping Sandy would get a sore head or tummy at some point on the trip to make it worthwhile me carrying it. Sandy carried the far more important things, the lights, the shifting spanner (a nice heavy one) and most critical of all, a half bottle of his "mystery malt" – the one which I need four glasses of before I can even hazard a guess at what it might be.

"Mmmm I'm not so sure, Sandy, can I just have a wee sip of that one again?"

When we are halfway up the sound of Mull, a good hour and a half into our six-hour journey, we descend to the cafeteria to go over our itinerary detail by detail. That done, it is back to stories about our holidays again.

Sandy had been touring the west coast of America and this had left him enthusing about the Grand Canyon. Visiting it was one of the top five things that he had wanted to achieve in his life. He wouldn't be persuaded to divulge what the other four were. Not this cycle trip I'm sure. He has recently become an enthusiastic scuba diver but was disappointed that he didn't have a chance to do this in America. "We just went to the aquarium instead." This reminded me of the story I heard many years ago of the American tourists being taken to Glasgow Airport for their homeward bound flight in the back of a Glasgow taxi. They told the driver that they were so disappointed that during their visit to Scotland they never got to see Loch Lomond. It was dark, so the helpful driver hatched a plan to make them achieve their wish. Half an hour later he was parked at the water's edge. "There you are – you can see it now." His passengers were thrilled and went home happy. Little could they have known that the well-meaning driver had taken them to the shores of Hogganfield Loch in one of Glasgow's parks.

I had also been slightly stymied during my holiday. We had been to Italy and visited Siena, home of the famous Pallio horse race. Unfortunately we arrived a day too late for the event, which involves the riders racing round the perimeter of the piazza three times. We were disappointed to miss it but thoroughly enjoyed watching the kids take a donkey ride the next day on a Mediterranean beach.

As we exit the Sound of Mull the Minch looks as calm as I have ever seen it. The light breeze is coming from the east, as it has been for the past week, and no swell has built up to affect the movement of the ship.

We have dinner on board - this will free up the evening when we get to Castlebay on Barra and possibly let us do a little bit of actual cycling.

The *Clansman* arrives on schedule (CalMac's timekeeping is very good I have to say) at Castlebay on Barra – island number one.

We cycle off the car-deck and up to our hotel. Apart from checking in we are very keen to find out if we can get to Mingulay tomorrow. It has a wild, romantic appeal to it and although cycling there is out of the question (just setting foot on it is hard enough) neither of us have been on it before and we are both very keen to get there. In fact we have a suspicion that it could turn out to be the highlight of the whole trip. The hotel manageress agrees and is very obliging.

"I'll phone the ferryman straight away for you."

By the time I lug my bags upstairs Sandy is already on the phone to him to hear the verdict. He looks serious.

It turns out that the boat to Mingulay is sailing at 10.30 tomorrow and holds ten people. It is full – but we are first on the cancellation list, and people often cancel at the last minute, once they see the height of the waves! So we are fairly optimistic as we return to our bikes.

After six hours on the ship we are desperate for a cycle – after all it is the reason that we're here. I have a plan. We should go to the neighbouring island of Vatersay tonight as we may not have time tomorrow. It should be an easy crossing for it is linked to Barra by a causeway. So we dump our panniers and other unnecessary clutter at our hotel before setting off.

After being cooped up on the ship we are keen to get off the leash, so once free of our panniers we're off like a couple of greyhounds released from their traps.

I think *I* am a fast cyclist but Sandy is a hundred metres ahead of me and flying at full pelt, before he looks round, sees I am not there and realises that he has been talking to himself for the last two minutes.

"What's keeping you?" he yells as I come puffing up to him.

The causeway linking Vatersay to its big sister Barra is two miles away from the little village of Castlebay. Halfway along the two miles there is a considerable climb uphill past the war memorial.

Vatersay is basically two hills, a big one and a wee one, joined by a thin band of land, running north to south, which has a beach on either side of it. The road circuits the eastern shores of the first hill and crosses the joining band to the small village at its end. The road from the causeway to the village is about three miles. The village looks a bit like a "job-lot" – wooden chalet-style houses grouped together, a couple of shops but no pub, unless it is hiding in someone's front room.

The air is very still, in fact the evening is surprisingly windless. I thought it was always windy, or at least breezy, in the Western Isles. Unfortunately this has a major side effect – midges in their thousands, indeed hundreds of thousands. They start biting at our faces – or rather my face. Perhaps they like my aftershave but they seem attracted to me and not Sandy. I can actually feel them biting, perhaps a dozen at a time. It is like the 1995 trip all over again.

We cycle up and down every road and track on Vatersay and then have a look at the beach on the eastern side. It is a beauty – empty but for a handful of gulls. I take this opportunity to give Sandy his first ornithological lesson, namely the difference between herring and common gulls, and how to identify a fulmar. I must admit that trying to enlighten him is hard going. As we head across the dunes I point out a gull flying past:

"Look! What's that?"

"It's a shag !"

I think he's being facetious.

We decide to cycle across a small field – to see what is on the other side. Corn buntings are singing their jangly song as we go. There is an open gate with a solitary brown cow barring the way. She seems friendly enough, however, and is happy to let us past.

On the other side of the field the west bay, known as Bagh Siar, is just as lovely, a generous strip of smooth yellow sand. Thousands of large, rounded, grey stones have been heaped up by the tide. Nearly all of them have beautiful black markings on them. They would look smashing around my garden pond.

"A fulmar!" screeches Sandy as a herring gull flutters by.

We head back across the field to the gate but to our horror the brown cow has been joined by about sixty-five of her mates, some with horns and they are all standing in front of the gate. Where the hell did they come from? They were nowhere to be seen five minutes ago. They have that look on their faces that says: "Do you dare to walk past us?" We push the bikes slowly past them making nice animal sounds like "moo" and "easy girls."

On the road back to Castlebay we pass a couple walking towards Vatersay whom we recognise as having been on the ferry with us earlier today. They are wearing nets over their heads – I hadn't realised they were that ugly but as we get nearer they turn out to be mosquito nets.

Grade One Amazonian mosquito nets. This is obviously serious midge country. When we get to our hotel it becomes clear why they needed them.

There are so many midges flying around in the still air that without them their faces would be eaten into mince by now.

The light is beginning to fade as we rush round the back of the hotel to park our bikes for the night. Our hurry to get inside away from the swarms is hampered by an Irish chap who is trying to unlock his bike from a lamppost but cannot remember the combination of his coded lock.

He has two options. Either he carries the lamppost about with him for the rest of his journey or he asks Sandy to help him. It takes my mathematician colleague all of forty seconds to work out the combination and free the bicycle. I wonder if he is that good at safes ?

In the bar to soak up a bit of Barra atmosphere. A band is playing some good old Celtic music and much foot-tapping and swilling of beer is going on; so we join in, particularly with the latter. I phone my family before retiring for the night. Their consensus is that they are "having the best holiday ever" – because I'm not there?

As we are sharing a room tonight Sandy promises that he will do his damnedest not to snore – something for which he apparently has a gift. I assure him that I am so tired that he will not disturb me. Exactly four minutes later there is a sound that I can most closely describe as what it must be like to have an Exocet missile enter through one wall of the room and go back out the opposite wall. And then it happens again . . . and again. . . .

Day One = 15 miles

Day 2 – Pabbay & Mingulay

TODAY THE WEATHER IS CRUCIAL. The forecast looked good but on wakening I'm rushing to open the curtains to see the real weather. It is bright, very bright, with a thin veil of broken high cloud. The breeze seems moderate – anything more than that and we will not get to Mingulay as the journey will be in an open boat for ten miles out into the Minch.

The weather is not the only factor, however. We do not even have places on the boat yet and will not unless somebody cancels.

Over breakfast we discuss the trip and are feeling optimistic. Sandy is to telephone the boatman at 10.00 to see if there is space. I, meanwhile, stick to what I'm good at – procuring a packed lunch, should he be successful in obtaining a place on the boat. It will be a long day if we go – not only does Mingulay not have a McDonalds – it is uninhabited as well.

Sandy makes the call. Bad news. No one has pulled out but we should get ourselves to the pier for 10.30 anyway. Then miracle of miracles, standing behind Sandy in the queue to use the phone are two girls who are waiting to phone the boatman to tell him that they no longer want to go. They overhear Sandy's conversation – *nosey things* – and are delighted to give us their places. Great stuff – we're off.

Sandy goes to tell the boatman and I confirm the need for the packed lunches: tomato and cheese sandwiches, crisps, apples, bottled water and a couple of cans of fizzy stuff – oh, and some sea-sickness tablets as well, just in case.

Down at the pier I can see no sign of any boat or passengers or Sandy. I can *hear* them, but I cannot see them. I peer cautiously off the end of the pier and there they are about four metres below me, already bobbing about in a small motor-boat on a low tide. I have to take the subterranean route under the pier to reach them.

We have eight fellow passengers. An English couple taking their third trip to Mingulay. A chap in his late-seventies making a lone pilgrimage, a lady from Barra with her two teenage daughters and two middle-aged, silver-haired sisters who have also done it all before. There is a crew of two on the boat, both of whom, I am relieved to observe, look as though they know what they are doing.

So what is so special about Mingulay that makes people want to bob about for several hours in a small boat to get there? I really don't know the answer to that one – so let's look at the geography and history to shed some light on it.

Mingulay is the second last of a chain of similar sized islands running south from Barra to form the bottom end of the Western Isles archipelago.

After Barra there is Vatersay, then Sandray, Pabbay, Mingulay and finally Berneray. From Castlebay on Barra to Mingulay is a distance of about ten miles, as the crow flies, but weaving our way today around the aforementioned islands we would cover a distance of some thirty-eight miles. In an open boat, with the minimum of cover from the elements, this journey would take about two and a half hours to get to Mingulay and the same to come back.

Mingulay itself is about three miles by two miles. The eastern, sheltered side has a kilometre-long stretch of golden beach and then the land gently curves up to the tops of the sheer cliffs that form the western edges of the island. The highest hills are Carnan to the west at 273 metres and Hecla to the south at 219 metres. The cliffs on the west side are almost as spectacular as those on St Kilda and almost as high. The highest are those at Biulacraig which rise sheer to a height of almost 250 metres (it sounds more impressive as 800 feet).

The remains of the village are still to be seen in the eastern bay. The village population reached one hundred and fifty by the 1880s but people eventually drifted away until the island was finally deserted in 1912. The ruins of the church and the school-house still stand defiantly at either end of the village. These isolated people survived from crofting, collecting sea-birds and their eggs and latterly by sheep farming.

There is one early story about a rent collector named Macphee that is worth recounting. One day he and his companions sailed to the island to collect the annual rent which was due to MacNeil of Barra. When he landed he discovered that the island's inhabitants were all dead and he rushed back to his boat and called to those onboard to get him off quickly as there was plague on the island. That was his big mistake for on hearing this his so-called friends turned the boat around as fast as they could and rowed off – leaving poor Macphee alone on Mingulay. Apparently he survived on the island for a year before it was deemed safe to evacuate him. MacNeil couldn't have been all bad however, for he apparently rewarded Macphee and his name was eventually given to the highest hill at the north end of the island. Nowadays, Mingulay and some of the neighbouring islands are owned by a group of Barra farmers who use them for sheep grazing. Apparently they are up for sale – let's hope they go to a good cause.

With great excitement back on our little boat we are about to make the epic journey. The sea looks calm and the light wind continues to blow from the east instead of the more prevalent south-west. A second, smaller motor-boat is tethered by a stout rope to our stern and as we turn to head away from the pier it falls away to five metres behind us as we take it in tow. I remark that it must be our lifeboat in case of emergency but the English chap who has done all this before shakes his head. "We use that to get ashore onto the rocks – there is no jetty, you see."

As we sail out into Castle Bay past Kiesmul Castle the *Clansman* comes running at speed into the bay on her morning call to Barra. Immediately we are hit by her wash and bounce energetically up and down for a few seconds. Great fun.

"That was good," I remark, but little do I know it is nothing compared to what is just around the corner.

The sea may look calm but as soon as we turn out of the bay the easterly wind takes its full effect on the sea and a moderate swell snatches at the boat constantly, causing us to pitch and roll our way out towards the eastern tip of Vatersay. The skipper is aiming for a gap in a malevolent looking reef just to starboard of a little island called Uinessan. The gap is barely seven metres across and we reduce speed to pass through it. The mate comes aft to where we are all sitting, out in the open rear area, to give us a few stories about the islands that we will be passing, but the noise from the waves and his soft, melodic brogue make most of his words drift idly past my ears without cognition.

The island of Muldoanich out to our left dissipates the effects of the wind and sea for a while but once past its influence, about forty minutes into the journey, we feel the full magnitude of their combined effect. Don't get me wrong – it is not rough and we all feel perfectly safe in our capable little boat but we do bob about a fair bit. I look aft and the boat we are towing is being alternately dragged back from us to the full extent of the rope and then hoisted high in the following surf to rise above us and charge towards our boat like a menacing piece of flotsam before falling back down again out of harm's way. The rope is being slackened then jarred and I notice that the skipper is regularly having a backwards look at it.

The other thing I notice is that the two teenage girls have lost their early chatter and have fallen a bit silent. Their expressions are becoming glummer with every heave the boat takes. Sandy and I are sitting at the stern and loving every moment of it all but I cannot help feeling a little guilty at enjoying an experience that is clearly beginning to take its toll on the morale of some others.

Sandy has sailed around most of Britain's coasts in various types of yachting craft and has even endured the twenty-four hour sail out to Mingulay's big brother – St Kilda. He has done all this without batting an eye or popping a pill. So I don't think he will suffer sea-sickness. I just hope I don't. So far I am feeling fine and my breakfast of bacon and scrambled eggs does not seem in any way perturbed by the motion of the boat – perhaps just a little more scrambled.

Not so the two young girls. By the time we have passed Sandray and are just off the eastern shores of Pabbay both are throwing up over the side of the boat. Fortunately not over my side. The skipper is understanding and decides to take the boat into the sheltered bay of Pabbay.

"Would anyone mind if we go ashore on Pabbay for half an hour?" It is clearly to give the girls a break and they look happier. I am delighted – Pabbay will be another island for us.

The boat is anchored and we haul ourselves into the smaller boat for a short 'phut – phut' across to the rocks guarding the beach. Seconds later, with helping hands all around we are ashore.

Pabbay is about a mile square and no longer inhabited. Sandy and I stroll up the shingle beach to find that the fertile ground between the low, rocky hillocks is a magnificent carpet of small wild flowers. I can swear that I have never seen so many beautiful wild flowers of such a variety of colours. Sandy swears that he has never seen so many butterflies. So we stand there, taking it all in, swearing at each other. Amongst the background greens there are dabbles of crimson, peach, yellow, delicate blues, lilacs – like a natural, three-dimensional impressionist painting. With the sun shining brightly on them the effect is simply stunning. We pick our way carefully across this carpet towards a ruined cottage where someone has laid out half a dozen sheep skulls on a derelict window ledge. Nearby there is a domed burial mound now covered in grass and flowers but still topped by a monolith.

We are joined by the two middle-aged sisters who have been here before. "I see we are not alone," says one of them pointing to a group of three olive-green tents sheltering in a little hollow nearby. I note a tinge of regret in her voice as she says it. "The skipper says there are six rock-climbers on the island, he brought them out in his boat three days ago. There are some fabulous cliffs on the south of the island."

Despite this intrusion into our own personal isolation (it is amazing how quickly one can get zealous about keeping some new found seclusion to oneself) we still have the feeling that nobody has ever set foot here before, ignoring the ruined buildings and burial-mound, of course. Sandy is already referring to me as Man Friday as I'm roaming about whistling the tune to that 1960s TV production of *Robinson Crusoe*. The two sisters are keen for a bit more solitude and opt to miss out Mingulay and stay on the island until we can pick them up again – in about six hours time !

So only eight of us head back to the boat. I wonder if the two girls will also opt out of the next bit but they are bravely back in their seats and are predictably turning green again as soon as we motor out through the Sound of Mingulay to reach the west side of our target island.

The skipper and mate intend to give us a treat. Instead of heading straight to the landing site on the east of Mingulay they are taking us on an anti-clockwise circuit of the island to let us see the steep western cliffs at close quarters. As this will be the sheltered side, unusually for the prevailing wind normally strikes from the south-west, they are taking advantage of a window of opportunity. The term "sheltered" is a euphemism as the sea on this side of Mingulay seems every bit as rough as on the other but within ten minutes we are below the cliffs and the views are so breathtaking that even the two girls have stopped being sick to gaze in wonder and even smile.

The highest cliff rises almost vertically out of the sea, its ledges covered in damp, short vegetation which gives it a matt greenish finish dotted in white from the nesting kittiwakes and fulmars. The boat is taken in close, to within seven metres sometimes, of the rocky stacks and pillars. Occasionally we are underneath some dark overhang. When we reach the isolated stack of Arnamul, the mate pulls our trailing boat in closer to our stern and we take a left turn in towards the cliff face. A narrow channel leads behind the stack to emerge on the other side. It seems impossibly narrow but we are steering towards it. As we squeeze through into the dark and dank channel between the stack and the island it is as if we have entered another world. Steep cliffs are all around us and only a thin shaft of grey light penetrates from the gaps in the cliffs many metres above us. The air is damp and the rocky walls echo with slopping and splashing from the unsettled water around us. Neither Sandy nor I have ever been anywhere like this before and it is almost a relief to emerge on the other side of the channel back into the open sea.

Further on, past more cliffs and reefs we turn around the south-western end of Mingulay and scrape delicately past a low shelf of rock with four large seals on it They lift their heads lazily and peer at us with a look that says, "You're not going to come so close that we're going to have to get up off this rock, are you?" They clearly cannot really be bothered so sit tight and let us go on our way.

I ask the mate how many times the conditions are suitable enough to allow him to sail as close to the cliffs as this, and around the channel behind the stack.

"Oh I'd say about two or three times a year."

We certainly are lucky chappies today. Sandy is so impressed that he reckons the experience is as enthralling as his recent visit to the Grand Canyon, and announces this to everyone on board. Now we have to look forward to actually landing on Mingulay and hopefully seeing the cliffs from the top of the island.

There is more excitement to come as we head across Mingulay Bay on the eastern side. We are only ten metres from the beach, for the sandy sea-bed shelves away quite steeply from the shore. As we drop anchor and prepare to step into the little boat which is bouncing like a Yo-Yo alongside us, a large dark shape appears in the clear water about seven metres away. A black dorsal fin sticks up from the water – perhaps about half a metre high. It is a basking shark and it has come to see what has disturbed the previously quiet bay. It swims around the boats for a couple of minutes, causing particular concern to one of our passengers. The skipper reassures her that it is harmless as it only eats plankton. I believe him but it takes a bit of trust when you see the eight foot mass of shark lingering with intent around our boats with its mouth gaping open. Let's hope it's not seen *Jaws*.

If getting ashore on Pabbay was tricky then landing on Mingulay is a bit like rock-climbing. There are no easy landing places here and we are on all fours trying to get up the rocky ledge onto the grass banks above. Once safely there, however, the view over the empty, golden, sandy beach brings home to us just how remote this island is.

We wander through the ruined village, with its abandoned school-house at one end and the derelict church at the other. A grass track, obviously man-made and elevated in places, served as the main street of the village but is now completely grass-covered. On either side the remains of the houses are clearly seen, most broken down to only a metre of wall in height. It must have been a hard, basic life here for the islanders and it is easy to see why they eventually gave up. I cannot blame them – but today in the sparkling clear sunshine and light, warm easterly breeze the beauty around us is breathtaking. So early in our trip, it is clear that this could be the highlight – just as we thought. It will take a major spectacle – like Sandy falling off his bike head first into a cowpat to beat it.

The eight landed passengers head off in their preferred directions, leaving the crew to doze away the three hours in peace while we explore the island. What else can they do for three hours? A good game of poker perhaps. Certainly there is the starboard side of the larger boat to be cleaned!

Sandy and I set off towards the ruins of the church, Sandy carrying our packed lunch in a gaudy Tennents Lager bag that makes him look as though he is taking a generous carry-out with him. We plonk our-selves down on a grassy knoll (quite unlike the one in Dallas, Texas) and stuff our faces with tomato and cheese sandwiches. The thought of spending three hours here seemed excessive at first – but now as we look around at our surroundings it seems too little time to take in the romance of Mingulay. Now I know why people try so hard to get here. A chap I had spoken to earlier on Castlebay said he knew someone who had come out to Barra three times over the last few years to get to Mingulay and had yet to succeed on account of the weather. We are very lucky chappies.

We have a discussion about what we want to do now. Our first target is to see the highest cliffs from their summit, so off we trudge, and it is a trudge, across bone dry moor and bracken to the western side of the island. Normally rough ground like this holds some kind of moisture, even during a dry summer. You know how it is; away from the road the hills look inviting until you start yomping across them and find that your trainers are soaked through and caked with mud after the first hundred metres. But here on Mingulay the ground is bone dry and even muddy puddles have become desiccated. Maybe this is not unusual on these windswept islands but the summer has been particularly good so far and the dryness is simply due to the low rainfall. Yet so many people are put off coming to places like this because they expect it to rain continuously.

As we near the top of the cliffs a dozen or so great skuas, bonxies, come into view. They eye us belligerently and soon take to the air. There are no nests or chicks around but it is inevitable that they will attack us, even if it is only to keep up their "cliff credit" with regard to the other seabirds and sure enough they do. Several kilograms of heavy beaked bird stooping towards you like a Stuka is rather off-putting – so I let Sandy go first and his arm-flailing seems to put them off.

After about twenty minutes climbing, good practice for the days of heavy cycling to come, we are at the top of the highest cliffs where the view down is giddying. I pose for a photograph.

"Get a bit nearer the edge," urges Sandy.

"You've got to be joking."

Sandy insists on reaching the summit of the highest hill which he feels cannot be far away. I plod along complaining behind him but to our surprise the summit is just over the next ridge. (For the rest of the trip he blames me for dragging him up to the top but I know my record of the facts is more accurate).

It is like sitting at the end of the world. To the north lie all the islands we have just sailed past, Castlebay clearly visible ten miles away. To the south lies Berneray with its lighthouse. But to the west, above the tops of the headlands and stacks way below us there is nothing but the cobalt blue Atlantic Ocean – looking spuriously benign.

We sit there for almost half an hour chatting in a desultory fashion. When one of us eventually looks at his watch we find that we only have fifty minutes left – and we still have the beach to visit, and hopefully a paddle, provided the shark has left.

All our fellow passengers are assembling at the beach when we get there and we swap stories about our Mingulay experiences. The couple who have been here twice before admit that this is their best trip so far – on account of the weather and being able to get close in to the rocks on the west side.

Our finned friend has gone but when I am splashing my hot feet around in the gentle surf a large grey seal surfaces remarkably close and has a good look at me. It could be days before they see another human, I suppose. As we leave the beach I glance back – all that is left of our visit are the footprints in the sand, stretching along the beach, where they will remain until the tide comes in.

Trying to get back into the wee boat is even more difficult than trying to get off it. The elderly chap is having a fair bit of difficulty getting one leg down in front of the other. Sandy tries hard to help him. I look on, trying to be helpful but merely getting in the way. I make my way down onto a different rock and look back at how Sandy is coping. When I see him with both hands on the old chap's buttocks I realise that perhaps it is best not to watch.

We head back to Pabbay to pick up the intrepid sisters. They have spent the day "swimming".

"I hope you weren't tempted to skinny-dip on the beach now." Sandy speaks his mind freely I am beginning to notice, but he asks the question with such sincerity that he gets away with it.

"Well we were a bit disappointed to find there were others on the island," says one of them with the merest tinge of red appearing on her already sun-tanned cheeks.

From the anchorage we turn back out around the southern shore of Pabbay and find a remarkable over-hanging rock formation coming into view with the six rock-climbers at various degrees of ascent (or descent – there is no way of telling) strung together by at least two ropes. I hope they know what they are doing for help is a long way away in the event of an accident. We wave – hoping that they are not daft enough to let go and wave back.

On again –- the sea seems a bit smoother now – or perhaps we are just getting used to it. Certainly the two girls seem to be enjoying the run home better than the run out this morning. One of them is even laughing at my attempts to brave it out in the open despite the fact that my efforts to dodge the incoming spray are worthless. Sandy positions himself with his back up against the cabin bulkhead, facing astern and is consequently the only one not showered in spray every few seconds, thus proving what an experienced sailor he is. I am sure all on board would admit it has been worth it. Anyone who is comfortable in a small boat for a few hours would have nothing to fear from going to Mingulay. For me it was an experience not to be missed.

We are back through the gap in the reef and onto Castlebay pier at six o'clock. What a wonderful day – but for us it is not over, we have to cycle round Barra now as it is the only chance we will have. At our hotel we leave our bags. The hotelier finds it incredible that having spent five hours at sea and three hours on Mingulay we should want to cycle round the island.

On the pier we bump into the two women who gave up their places for us on the boat. They had seen the boat returning and have come down to hear our tales. Although Sandy and I extol the virtues of the journey and our experiences on the two islands they look unconvinced and seem relieved that they did not go.

Round the island anticlockwise to get the big climb out of Castlebay over first. Sandy does not like hills – name a cyclist who does! He growls at a couple of sheep as he hauls himself out of the saddle and strains at the pedals. I don't know what influence a couple of sheep are having on his efforts but he seems to like giving them verbal abuse.

At the top he stops to get his breath back. "Look at me, I'm in a lather."

The road undulates around the fourteen-mile circuit of Barra. About halfway around my front derailleur (gear changer) snags and I have to do a quick adjustment. I have a sinking feeling that all is not well with it – and the cycling has hardly begun ! On the far western side at Hogh Bay we arrive at a hotel at 20.55 and hope to grab a bite to eat and watch the sun slipping off the end of Scotland into the sea. We are lucky to get a meal at all as the barman checks the clock three times while taking our modest order – just in case it is after nine pm, in which case we would be too late.

We also have to keep an eye on the time as the *Lord of the Isles* is due in at Castlebay at 22.00 and we have to load our bikes and gear onboard before she shuts up her car-deck for the night. Our beds for the night are on board. So we continue our circle and return to the hotel where our bags are being kept for us.

We are just in time, our ship is arriving as we gather our stuff from the hotel and we cycle up the ramp onto the capacious car-deck just before they close it up for the night. The ship will sail at 05.00 tomorrow morning for Mallaig and then Armadale, where we will be getting off.

A word to the chief steward so that he does not wake us too early and we have a quick dram from Sandy's *Guess the Malt* bottle in one of the lounges. Although we are free to come and go as we please from the ship neither of us feels like going back up to the hotel.

"We could have a great ceilidh in here," says Sandy. Fine. There are just the two of us. All that sea air is obviously affecting his brain. We retire to our cabins and the steady thud of the generator which seems to be above my head if not quite inside it.

Day Two = 14 miles

Total for two days = 29 miles

DAY 3 – SKYE & ISLEORNSAY

I AM STIRRED FOR THE UMPTEENTH TIME from my slumbers by a change in tone from the engine above me. We seem to be on the move – so it must be at least 05.00. I feel as though I haven't slept at all – but I've probably slept quite well. At least the bunk is warm and cosy. I turn over and fall back asleep again. During the three and a half hour passage to Mallaig I am aware of a gentle rocking and creaking of the ship but this is actually quite soothing.

A knock on my door wakes me again and I glance at my watch. It is almost 09.00. I wash and dress in record time and surface on deck. The chief steward has changed into a different person and I look at him with an air of puzzlement.

"Where are we?" It seems such a silly question but I feel that it has to be asked.

"Just about ten minutes from Mallaig – we're running a wee bit late on account of the tide."

The ship is due to turn around quickly at Mallaig and reach Armadale on Skye at 09.30. Good – time for my breakfast. I stuff into bacon and eggs and tea alone in the restaurant – no idea where Sandy is, he would only disapprove anyway, but I know he is up and about somewhere. We eventually bump into each other on deck as the ship is docking at Mallaig. Nocturnal reminiscences are exchanged and are unsurprisingly similar.

The weather is yet again bright and sunny and a very interesting cycle now awaits us on Skye. We are sailing over to Armadale, catching up on lost time. Armadale is on the Sleat peninsula, the long, narrow point of land that juts southwards from the main body of Skye. We intend cycling a circular route out over the hills to the west side of the peninsula and then back over to the eastern side on a different road. It is a part of Skye less frequently visited and neither of us has cycled there before. With the good weather it augurs well for a great morning of cycling.

By lunch time we should have completed about three-quarters of the circle and we may then visit the little hamlet of Isleoransay with its tidal island and lighthouse. If our luck is in – and it usually is – the tide will be out and we can visit the island.

The *Lord of the Isles* has made up time and arrives on schedule at Armadale. We will join her later in the afternoon and again tomorrow evening.

A mile out on our route we find a pile of large cut logs, slightly off the road and decide to dump our panniers here so that we can cycle light. We take our toolbag with us – that remains strapped to the bike at all times – and a few snacks gleaned from the cafeteria of the ship.

We turn left uphill on the quiet road towards Tarskavaig.

The road climbs to 188 metres over just two miles, probably the highest and steepest climb of our entire trip – although there is one a few days ahead of us on Harris that I am already previewing in trepidation. Halfway up two military jets roar out of the blue over an adjacent hill towards us and drop down to scream over the valley below. We seem to be higher than they are. They turn out at sea to come around and roar past us again.

Hopefully they are not using my red fleece or Sandy's red shorts as target practice. The pilot's view of the scenery on a sparkling sunny morning such as this must be a joy. But we will soon earn ourselves a decent view when we get to the top of the hill.

A bit further on, Sandy is moaning at the sheep again – and there aren't any sheep there. "I'm in a lather!" he complains as if someone has showered him in soap suds.

I have noticed that he tackles hills in a completely different way from me. I tend to plod along at a steady rate, not over-exerting myself in case I go into cardiac arrest. Sandy, on the other hand, takes out a personal vendetta on each hill. He treats each incline like an enemy or like someone who owes him money with whom he has to get even and he strains onwards, actually going faster than he does when on the flat. He subsequently overtakes me as he raises himself out of the saddle muttering under his breath:

"I'll get you, you . . . !" or "You'll not get the better of me, you . . . !"

When he gets annoyed with hills like this, and when he is wearing his baseball cap and sunglasses, and with his newly acquired moustache I can swear he looks and sounds like Kevin Kline from *A Fish Called Wanda*. When I tell him this he gets even more annoyed: "I'll get you Craig!" And so, on each hill we come to, all I get is a view of Sandy's substantial red-shorted backside lurching from side to side as he battles with his rakish adversary. Needless to say he is waiting for me at the top – glowing in victory and sweating profusely.

"Look at me – I'm in a lather." This time proudly.

From the top of the hill we have a wonderful view of the Cuillins – Black and Red – and the Strathaird peninsula of the island.

The downhill prize is so fast that I am cold when we finally pull to a halt at Tarskavaig Bay. My skin temperature must have dropped by about 15C from the top of the hill to the bottom.

We don't hang around but push on to the start of the downhill at Gauscavaig where we stop for five minutes so that I can eat a sandwich or three.

"You can't be hungry already?" exclaims Sandy who is constantly bemused by my regular eating.

"I had a rushed breakfast on the ship and that was hours ago – well about an hour ago," I explain.

I need the energy, because the climb from Tokavaig, a mile further on, is a killer which even has me cursing. In fact, to be honest, on the first bit we both get off and push – there is nothing in the rule book which says you can't push. The road undulates here, which is tiring. The bike is either doing three or thirty-three miles per hour. In fact I prefer a long steady climb to all those steep up and downs – which is just as well for there is another long steady climb just round the next bend as we head back across Sleat to the east side. It is such an attractive road, however, that we don't mind too much. From Loch Meodal to the main-road there is a lovely downhill. At the bottom, instead of going right back to Armadale, we turn left and head for Isleornsay where we fancy we might treat ourselves to a bar lunch.

Another climb, and into the wind, but the road surface is fast and we keep up a good pace. Just beyond the summit a male hen harrier glides past us and starts to hunt low over the fields to our left. It is a fine sight but one which is lost on Sandy, who is convinced it is only a gull.

Isleornsay is a delightful little village with a handy shop (shut) and hotel (open). The bikes are dropped outside and we grab a quick baked potato lunch washed down with a beer. We have covered eighteen decidedly hilly miles and vote not to venture any further north – we shall be seeing much more of Skye later in the week, so why bother now. As the tide is out, although on the turn, we decide to make for the tidal island of Ornsay – on foot. There is, after all, a rather interesting-looking lighthouse at the end of the island – if we can make it that far in the time available.

The route across to Ornsay is over a couple of muddy beaches and we are soon slipping about on them. We are aware that the tide is rising but it seems to be rising very slowly. Sandy gives me a mathematical lecture on what percentage of the tide rises with each hour. It is all he can do to stop himself scribing a histogram or pie-chart on the mud. This is what I get for trying to teach him some ornithology.

After about fifteen minutes we can rightfully claim to be standing on Ornsay and so head further out to cross another tidal portion of it towards the lighthouse.

The lighthouse was built in 1857 and is a prominent feature of the Sound of Sleat (well, I suppose it would be, wouldn't it!) There is a dwelling house adjacent to it which looks occupied, so we don't peer in the windows. We walk gingerly around the lighthouse and then perch on a big boulder at the water's edge. After about five minutes a young chap appears as if from nowhere, but presumably the house and approaches us.

"I thought I'd better tell you that you have only about forty-five minutes to get back to the mainland before the tide cuts you off."

We thank him for his kind advice. "That was very decent of him," says Sandy.

"Yes, but he doesn't want to have to put us up for the night."

We head back – and sure enough, the water is rising steadily around us. For a few minutes until I can just see the rocky causeway which we crossed earlier I begin to wonder what it would be like spending the night on these few acres of island – too embarrassed to knock the resident's door and admit we screwed it up and could we have dinner – with a nice bottle of chilled Chablis – bed and breakfast please?

Back at Isleornsay we sit on the jetty and watch as the water rises at a rate of eight centimetres every ten minutes. Forty-five minutes after the chap at the lighthouse had issued his warning the route across the muddy beach is obscured by the rising tide – and we had thought he was exaggerating.

The moral is simple – always heed a local's advice on such matters. We are pleased to claim Ornsay as yet another island. After all we have this chap as our witness to our visit.

There is a ferry due to leave Armadale for Mallaig at 16.00 and we decide to catch it rather than wait for a later one, so we retrace our steps – or should I say our tread – up the hill, followed by a very swift descent, with a tailwind, towards Armadale.

By now I have come to accept that the front derailleur on my bike is not right, in fact it is seriously wonky and I, which means we, are going to have to look at it tonight during our evening stop-over at Mallaig.

Our bags are where we left them, surprise ! surprise ! We make our return sailing on the *Lord of the Isles* and on arriving at the mainland seek out our hotel, which is only a stone's throw away from the harbour. It is a very comfortable establishment indeed and we plan to dine there tonight – mainly because there is sea bass on the menu and sea bass to me is like candy to a baby. In my fishy experiences it is second only to wild salmon as the nicest beast to come out of the sea.

Before all that we decide to take a walk around the town, which takes all of three minutes. "What will we do now ?" asks Sandy.

We consider having another cycle but it really is hot now and we decide to chicken out and save our mainland cycling for tomorrow, after our trip to Eigg. I have some clothes to wash and ask politely if the hotel can dry them for me by tomorrow afternoon when we shall be finally leaving Mallaig. To cut down the weight that I have to carry in my panniers I only brought five sets of clothes for the eight days, knowing there I would be time to have some laundered here in Mallaig. That's planning for you.

So after a busy half hour over the wash-hand basin I rejoin Sandy at the harbour to see what the local fishermen have caught. Only one boat

boat comes in while we are there and it lands a dozen boxes of langoustines, all pink beady-eyed and crawling. After another half hour of this we have an appetite and there is nothing else for it but the sea bass, washed down with just a little wine.

Suitably refreshed we head out to the back yard of the hotel to our bikes and get the tools out in a joint effort to fix my front derailleur.

It all starts simply enough. First the locking bolt needs tightening, I know that already, but then my cycling pal suggests that we dismantle the mechanism and inspect it. Emboldened by half a bottle of Chilean Sauvignon Blanc I foolishly agree - and find that I cannot get it back together again. By now my hands are smeared in oil, which is fair enough but I also need the toilet. I return to the hotel, leaving behind oleaginous light switches, a black mark on the front of my trousers and . . . well . . . worse !

Back to the bike where Sandy has taken control and is suggesting I completely dismantle my bike and rebuild it again. He has discovered a broken metal lug, only a couple of millimetres across, which is responsible for screwing up my front gears. But he has a solution, like all good maths teachers.

"I've got it – you need to buy a circlip to hold on the mechanism – either that or a new bike."

We've been bent over the bike for more than an hour, dismantling more things, accumulating nuts and bolts and gradually making the problem worse. I am getting oilier and oilier; but not Sandy who miraculously seems to be as clean as a whistle, and now we are being guzzled alive by midges. So we decide to leave my bike disabled for the night and see if we can buy a circlip at the ship chandlers in the morning before heading out to Eigg. If we don't have time to fix it in the morning we can always use the time on the boat. I go off to clean my hands, and other parts, and render the hotel light-switches as good as new again.

The remainder of the evening is spent having a look into the local pubs, just a look, we don't actually go into any.

Tonight we are sharing a room but it is just nice to fall asleep in a bed that is not rising and falling and not have two Mirrlees Blackstone engines reverberating in my head – but then Sandy hasn't started snoring yet.

Day Three = 25 miles

Total for three days = 54 miles

DAY 4 – EIGG & SOUTH UIST

IT IS 04.00 AND A RABBLE OF GULLS ON THE ROOF outside our room are giving it *laldy*. God knows what they are up to at that time of the morning. "What kind of gulls are they, Sandy?" I sleepily mutter.

"Flying gulls!"

When I wake for the final time it is to another clear blue sky. Being health conscious in our eating habits breakfast is the usual unhurried affair with our menus carefully chosen so as to provide the necessary nutrition, bearing in mind the labours ahead of us, without unduly over-loading the digestion. In other words bacon, fried egg, sausages, black pudding, fried mushrooms, toast, butter and tea for me and a glass of ice-cold milk (full fat of course) for Sandy. Yumm.

Now it is off to the ship's chandlers to procure a narrow circlip for my bike. I buy one and we try it eagerly around the wounded bit of frame. It is too wide. I had noticed a small ship repair yard down at the harbour yesterday so we take the bike and the circlip down to see if someone can be bothered to machine it to the correct width. A kind chap in greasy dungarees can. He obligingly grinds a few millimetres off the width until it fits the mechanism. He seems interested in our trip, especially when he hears that we are catching the ship to Eigg in just a few minutes.

"Never been to Eigg," he says, "I'm a Muck man myself."

I don't quite know how to take this.

"I mean I was *born* on Muck," he adds, sensing the confusion caused by his last statement. We reward him with the price of a pint and head off to find our ship to Eigg, which leaves from the pier in fifteen minutes.

The *Lochmor* is the vessel which will deposit us on Eigg for two hours.

We wheel onboard and while everyone else (including Sandy) sits down to enjoy the hour and a half cruise out to the island I get the sleeves rolled up and set about fixing my front gear with my custom-milled circlip. I have to borrow a hacksaw and a hammer from the bosun (just in case I have to use force) and a plastic cup full of Swarfega cleaning agent for my poor hands. Sandy sits and looks on, nodding his head encouragingly but not daring to get his own hands dirty.

After toiling for fifteen minutes I get the circlip on only to find that although the derailleur is now secure – which was, after all, the original problem – it will no longer 'deraill'. It just isn't going to work. Sandy comes up with a whole new set of ideas and instructions but he sees my long-suffering look and backs down. I will have to abandon the derailleur altogether but will have to break the chain first to get it off.

Out comes my little chain-splitting tool – a useful, indeed excursion-saving, device if ever there was one. I have to push one of the rivets linking the chain through to one side without popping it completely out the other side. My hands now look as if I have just immersed them in a bath of crude oil and I doubt if they will ever be clean again. Practically everyone onboard the little ship seems to be leering over my shoulder watching to see if I make a dog's breakfast of it. There! I get it split, remove the derailleur and put it back together again only to discover, to my horror, that I have inadvertently put a kink into the chain and will have to do it all over again. Meanwhile a glance over the bulwarks shows that Eigg is now only a few minutes away – it looks as though I'm going to be walking on the island instead of cycling.

However, by keeping a cool head I repeat the whole riveting process, successfully once again, without the kink this time. I can now cycle using my six rear gears only and if I come to a steep hill then I can stop and push the chain onto a smaller (lower) gear with a finger. All this because I needed to tighten a bolt!

The *Lochmor* serves the 'Small Isles' of Rum, Canna, Muck and Eigg in different combinations each day. Only Canna has a pier, so a small tendering vessel has to come out to meet the ship as it anchors out in the Bay. It is an absorbing experience watching the diligence with which the crew of both boats safely transfer the passengers and all their accoutrements from one boat to another and then ashore. About thirty passengers are heading for the island along with us but we are the only ones with bikes and I can sense a couple of people looking at us with a touch of envy; we will be able to see a fair bit of the island in the two hours whereas most of the others will not have time to get far from the pier.

Our bikes are placed on top of the red-hulled motor-boat, which is called the *Ulva*. We set off away from the *Lochmor* towards the jetty on the island. I sit deep into the little cabin which has a hatch opening onto the bow. A small lad of about eight, looking remarkably like my own son Tony, is sitting up on the bow adjacent to me, helping with the rope.

Looking at him suddenly gives me a pang of homesickness. A screeching overhead brings me out of my reverie and I peer out to see what the din is. Above the boat a party of about a dozen arctic terns are being harried by a large female peregrine falcon. Then as I look more closely I see that it is actually the other way round – it is the terns that are doing the harrying, chasing the peregrine as she heads out across the sea towards the mainland.

There is a family group of French people onboard, including some small children. I see a perfect opportunity to practise my considerably inept French; a habit I have, much to my family's embarrassment, even in non-French places, such as Sauchiehall Street. A little girl is needing a seat so I raise myself out of mine and offer it to her.

"Asseyez-vous, s'il vous plait." I'm quite pleased with myself – a whole sentence!

She looks at me in bewilderment but sits down anyway. Her mum notices and leans over to me. "Thank you, but she is actually from Paisley."

Eigg is a small island belonging to the group loosely known as 'The Small Isles' which also comprises Muck, Rum and Canna. Its former Gaelic name (Eilean Nimban More) meant "the island of the big women". The island is roughly heart shaped, about five miles by four. There are a couple of small communities, one at the south-east, where the ferry anchors, and one at the north. The island has a backbone of cliffs running down the eastern side but its most obvious geographical feature is the isolated four hundred metre high plug of volcanic rock called An Sgurr. This pillar dominates the south end of Eigg and can be seen from miles around.

Another geographical feature but with a grim history is Macdonald's cave, near to the landing jetty, which I am keen to see. It was the scene of an atrocity of almost biblical proportions back in 1577. The locals (MacDonalds) had been having a few run-ins with the MacLeods of Skye over their women folk. After sending the MacLeods packing, and some-what mutilated in a particularly sensitive area, the Skye clan decided to retaliate and sent over an assault force. When they discovered two hundred MacLeods hiding in the cave they laid fires at the entrance and the billowing smoke suffocated every poor soul inside.

The recent history of Eigg is almost as turbulent. The island pros-pered under several landlords after being sold by the MacDonalds in 1829 but by the early 1980s the islanders were in dispute with the then owner Schellenberg. He left and relations did not improve when the German Maruma took over. Finally in 1997 the island was successfully purchased for the islanders themselves after the setting up of a trust.

Their future now lies in their own hands – all eighty pairs of them – but much work has to be done; there is no mains electricity and no proper pier for the ferry. We will be landed by tender and are very keen to get ashore – to see if the island is still populated by "big women". There is certainly a very large one standing on the jetty.

Looking at the map we decide to cycle northwards along the road for as far as it goes. Then, if we have time, we can visit the cave.

We set off along the narrow metalled track which serves as the road and which runs up the middle of the island. After a steep hill as it curves away from the shore the road levels out for its length of four miles before petering out. This is all new territory for both of us and it is a delightful cycle, travelling light, save for the tool bag.

At each house along the way the 'thud-thud' of diesel generators is evident which must destroy the peace somewhat for the islanders. Perhaps National Grid electricity will arrive one day. Eigg strikes me instantly as a beautiful island - one of the nicest I have ever seen, and I have seen a few now. To our left natural deciduous and coniferous woods reach up to An Sgurr while coming up on our right are the steep jagged eastern escarpments. Further on a softer landscape falls away to the sea in a patchwork of small fields of dazzling greens and ochres dotted with white walled crofts. And just across the sea there is the lumpy dark form of the island of Rum. It is a strikingly gorgeous scene, given that extra polish by the glistening sunshine.

We've already used up half of our allotted time ashore so plonk ourselves down at the end of the road to eat our lunch and rave to each other about how wonderful the scenery is. All the other visitors who came ashore with us are missing this because they didn't bring their bikes with them.

With just over half an hour remaining we head back along the road. A puncture for one of us now could mean us missing the boat and having to stay here until Thursday, so we keep an eye out for sharp stones.

Back at the jetty a group of people are standing around outside the cafeteria where there is a map of the island housed in a frame. We take a look at the map to see if we have time to visit the infamous cave. The boatman is sitting outside enjoying a mug of coffee and I ask him if we have time to see it. He shakes his head.

"It's too far to walk there and back in fifteen minutes, and you could do with a torch in any case."

"It will have to wait for another trip then," I reply.

"Yes," he nods. "Don't forget the torch."

As we speak a helicopter roars across the bay and swings round to touch down on a patch of flat grass just behind the cafeteria. Nobody around me bats an eye.

We have ten minutes so after swilling down a refreshing mug of tea we head up the road that leads to the Big House which once housed all the most recent lairds, but not at the one time, and which now stands empty. We find it up a rocky track about a mile from the jetty. It has an Italian style which seems out of character for the island and looks as if it is about to commence the slow, inevitable path to decay. I notice that the front garden of the house is completely enclosed by a tight ring of rhododendrons which block out all view of the bay. Shame to live on such a lovely island and not have a view of the sea. Maybe that's why the house is empty.

At the jetty the loading and unloading process goes into reverse. It is a real eclectic bunch waiting to get on the little boat. Most of the intending passengers came out with us this morning but a few are missing and others are new. A couple of other bikes and their owners are waiting, a chap with two oil drums which he obviously wants to take back to the mainland and a little old lady wearing a rather oddly shaped hat and with a little yapping dog on a lead. There is also a young couple having a tearful parting, their doleful gazes into each other's eyes interrupted by long uninhibited kisses.

The boat has to take two trips out to the *Lochmor* so we hang back for the second one. I look back with a hint of sadness at the island receding behind us – I'll have to come back here for a proper visit one day. I'm not half as sad as the young girl, however, who is waving forlornly to her boyfriend who has remained on the jetty, tears rolling down her sun-tanned cheeks. It is amazing the friendships that can be forged in a two-hour visit.

On the sail back to Mallaig we compare our bike computer readings. The odometer readings for our cycle on Eigg are not the same - they should be. I realise that the new slimmer tyres fitted to my bike before the start of the trip are not calibrated to the computer and I am getting readings that are too high – by about twelve per cent. Judging by the map, the distances we have covered seem to be accurately recorded on Sandy's computer, so we will have to use his from now on to record the all important tally at the end of each day.

It is still early afternoon when we arrive back at Mallaig so rather than hang about trying to see if we can fix any other parts of my bike which don't need fixing we head straight out of town to the first white sandy beach we can find. There are lots of them along this part of the west coast and we know that we won't have to go far to find one. About three miles in fact, just past Morar.

We dump the bikes and paddle around up to our knees in the turquoise water of a little inlet bounded on all sides by the most brilliant white sand. Lots of other people are paddling around as well so I don't feel too silly. On examination they are all about three years old. After all that hard cycling (a whole twelve miles today!) this is the reward. Sandy wanders off through the water around the corner into another little bay and I stand alone, like Robinson Crusoe, dreaming of my next ship – the *Lord of the Isles* to Lochboisdale in about an hour.

Man Friday comes splashing back around the corner and we get back on our machines and head for Mallaig. For once it is Sandy who is dilly-dallying and I take the chance to push on ahead on the long straight section of new road past Morar.

I remember to collect my dried washing from the hotel – they have dried and folded it so neatly for me and for no charge. I stuff it into my pannier and rendezvous with Sandy outside the fish and chip shop. He has been determined since arriving in Mallaig yesterday to have a fish supper. He ladles fistfuls of battered haddock down his throat in great delight.

"I thought we were going to have dinner on the ship ?" I enquire.

"Mmnn . . . we are," he splutters.

The *Lord of the Isles* arrives on time and we board the car-deck with our bikes, showing our Island Rover tickets. By now we are beginning to be recognised – with an air of puzzlement. Indeed we are off to cross the Minch for the third time in four days.

We have a beer and get talking to a couple of the crew who seem genuinely interested in our travels. They appear to like their jobs and Sandy asks one of them how he manages to sleep with the noise of the generator or engines overhead.

"There is an X drawn on the car-deck," he explains, "my bunk lies directly below it and that's where they drop all the anchoring chains at three o' clock in the morning when I'm in my bunk." He continues, "No seriously, I sleep like a log on the ship, it's when I go home I find trouble – my wife has to throw buckets of water at the outside of our bedroom window to get me to sleep."

We ask if we can go up to the bridge and permission is granted. What a wonderful view we have from up there. The skipper and mate seem to be having a whale of a time – literally – spotting dolphins, porpoises and indeed a distant minke whale as we sail out past the island of Canna. Meanwhile the satellite navigation system is steering the *Lord of the Isles*. Visibility is very clear and the view all around from our exalted position is magnificent. Away ahead the distant lumps of South Uist, our destination, can be clearly seen. We spend almost a half hour up there.

Sandy is in his element. "Look at that lovely yacht over there, isn't she creaming along just a treat?"

The highlight is when a school of at least twenty dolphins appears on the port side of the ship, just astern of us. They leap and jump randomly from the water causing it to look as though it is boiling. At any one moment at least one of them is in the air. The captain reckons they are becoming a commoner sight.

The ship slips stealthily past the hills guarding the entrance to Lochboisdale at 21.45, as the last of the day's light fades gently from the sky, leaving behind the most enchanting mother-of-pearl sky.

The next bit promises to be fun. We have to find our way to our bed and breakfast cottage with only one set of lights between us – another weight economy. So Sandy takes the front light and I take the rear and we cycle very close together, one behind the other. Sandy has stayed in this B n' B before and highly recommends it. Our beds are booked, the only problem is he cannot remember where it is. Somewhere between Lochboisdale and Lochmaddy, he reckons. Wonderful !

We pedal away from the *Lord of the Isles* for the last time on our trip – we've actually become quite attached to her as she is a very comfortable ship. Sandy leads the way and we immediately find the north-easterly wind helping us along. Various trucks and cars from the unloading ship fly past us as a multitude of bungalows appear at the roadside on either side.

"Which one is it, Sandy ?"

"It's just up here, I promise."

Two miles further on: "It's this next one, I'm certain it is. No, no it's not that one." Another two miles pass by and still we are pedalling in close harmony.

"There it is – it's this one. Oh, wait a minute, no I don't think it's that one either. Maybe it was the one a mile or two back . . ."

We eventually find it. It is quite obvious really – all the lights are on inside it and there is a friendly black sheep-dog waiting at the end of the driveway for us. It is more a Saint Bernard that we are in need of.

Sandy was right. It is a very comfortable house but we decline the offer of a cup of tea for something a little stronger. The bags are dumped and we cycle on another mile to the local hotel where we share the next half-hour with the barmaid and a hydrologist up on the islands on survey work for the proposed causeway linking South Uist to Eriskay.

It seems as though all the Western Isles will soon be one big causeway. We chat about the eclipse of the sun which is due tomorrow and I realise for the first time that even this far north the moon's coverage of the sun will still be as high as seventy per cent. If the sky is free from cloud we will have a good chance of seeing it – at around 11.15. Our minds are on other meteorological features as well. Should the wind remain from the north-east it is going to be a long, hard cycle tomorrow for the fifty miles to Lochmaddy on North Uist. Tomorrow is the day of the longest cycle of the entire trip and we are rather hoping that the normally prevailing south-westerly wind will indeed prevail. We will just have to wait and see.

The ride back to the guest-house is in total darkness, once we leave the street-lights behind. The wind in our faces is chilly but invigorating. Let's hope we find it invigorating in our backs tomorrow.

Day Four = 23 miles

Total for four days = 77 miles

Day 5 – South Uist, Orosay, Benbecula, Grimsay, Baleshare & North Uist

WAKENED AT 05.00 BY A BEWILDERED SHEEP baahing outside our open bedroom window. It's a different noise that wakes me each morning. Gulls yesterday and diesel engines the day before that. Is it impossible to get a decent sleep in these places ?

This is the day of the Big Cycle, from the bottom half of South Uist to the top half of North Uist. It is actually the first time that we are heading in a straight line from A to B, as it were, fully laden with our panniers and stuff. No nice wee circular day trips or boat trips today, this is us now progressing in a northerly direction under our own steam. For the rest of the trip we will have to pedal – pedal – pedal.

Measured on the map our route today will add up to forty-three miles but no doubt there will be diversions on the way which will raise the mileage considerably. So the important thing today is the weather – or more specifically the wind direction. Normally this is from the south or south-west which would suit us just fine, for we could get ourselves along without pedalling a stroke. So far this week the wind has been from the east – which has a kind a neutral effect if cycling south to north. Another slightly important factor would be a lack of rain. Our route today is particularly exposed. So I step outside before breakfast to take in the conditions. It is the sunniest morning so far – but the wind has moved to the north-east which means we will get it on the nose all the way north. Not much we can do about that – we'll have to pedal every stroke.

Wind direction is a crucial factor with regard to the energy used on a cycle. A hill is no more than ten or fifteen minutes work but a constant head wind is very tiring because it is unrelenting. So I am a little concerned as we will be heading directly into the wind for almost fifty miles and I do not have my full range of gears. I could of course let Sandy go ahead of me and try sheltering behind him. What a pity we don't have a tail-wind. I remember once setting off from Craigmore on Bute to Rothesay with a gusting wind behind me and arriving at Rothesay pier three minutes later without having pedalled a single stroke. The wind pushed me from behind with such force that I had to constantly brake. No such luck today.

It is also a very important day today for astronomical matters. 11 August 1999, the day Sir Patrick Moore has awaited for most of his long life – the first total solar eclipse of the sun to be seen in Britain for seventy years. Sir Patrick himself is on breakfast telly practically dancing from one leg to another in excitement. The roads to the West Country of England are crammed with cars for this much hyped event. Here on South Uist we will have the roads almost to ourselves when the event occurs at 11.15. There is a down side, of course (there always is). Our Hebridean eclipse will only be about seventy per cent, that is to say only seventy per cent of the sun's face will be covered by the moon. However, we have a clear blue sky this morning whereas Cornwall is heaving under cloud, so we fancy that our chances of seeing something of the main star attraction (excuse the pun) may be pretty good. But to tell you the truth we are more interested in our cycle, and the most interesting thing of all at this moment is our breakfast.

It is a monumental affair – the size of all of the previous days' breakfasts put together: sausages, bacon, black pudding, white pudding, tomatoes, eggs, mushrooms etc. etc. What Sandy refers to as "the full horror". That is not all – the packed lunches we ordered the night before are equally generous and consequently add considerable weight to our bags – but at least that weight is likely to diminish the further north we go.

We are on the road at 09.20 but turn our bikes southwards for a small detour before the big hike north. We have spotted a nice little tidal island called Orosay on the south-west corner of Uist, some five miles away. It will be an interesting diversion, and the tides should be just right for us to tick another island.

By our book tidal islands (islands which are completely surrounded by the seas at high tide only) count as full islands if they are a good bit more than a rock and if they have a name. There are some famous ones; Oronsay linked to Colonsay, for instance and, probably the most famous of them all, Lindisfarne, or Holy Isle, linked to the Northumberland coast. The actual size is not important, as long as they are named on the map. This one seems to take the biscuit as it beckons at us from the map. You may have noticed by now that such tidal islands all seem to be called Oronsay or a corruption of that name - Isleornsay that we visited on Skye two days ago in addition to the other examples named above. The name *Ornsay* or *Oronsay* or *Oransay* is the old Norse name for a tidal island which is joined to the mainland at low tide. There are about twenty of them in Scotland – this will be our second this week.

With the wind briefly behind us we cycle along quiet roads past fields that are being farmed in the traditional, less intensive way and accordingly are embroidered with wild flowers of the most beautiful delicate colours in a manner rarely seen now on the mainland. The variety is as stunning as we saw on Pabbay. I wish I could name them but my total knowledge of things botanical could be mown onto the face of a daisy. I really don't know an iris from a gladiolus, which at the moment I rather regret. There are fields of hay and oats, some already harvested and some actually being harvested as we cycle past. Old fashioned domed hay-stacks fill a small field to our right as we turn down to Orosay. Lapwings, a declining bird on the mainland, are everywhere and flocks of buzzing twite dash from stubble field to stubble field. These are really meadows, not fields. When we stop to check our map a farmer turning cut hay in the field, sorry – meadow, next to us comes over to pass the time of day with us, well, five minutes of it anyway. He grows the hay as winter feed for his own cattle munching away in the next kaleidoscopic meadow. When we ask him about the eclipse he shrugs. "So what!" That is what I like about the islanders. They are friendly and accommodating and totally underwhelmed and unaffected by such media trivia as the first total solar eclipse for seventy years.

At the narrow strip of beach connecting Orosay to South Uist the tide is parting sportingly for us and we dump the bikes and trample across the shingle and up the grassy slope of our two-acre island. We don't pace it out or anything like that, it just looks about two acres, which is roughly the size of Glasgow's George Square. It is really just a grassy mound but we bound up to the top of it anyway. Once there Sandy makes me climb up onto a huge boulder so he can take my photograph. He keeps asking me to perform these stunts in exposed places. I believe he actually hopes I fall off while he is clicking the shutter release button and consequently gets himself the 'photo of the month' award from the *Sunday Times*. In which case he is dis-appointed yet again.

Any thoughts that we are just being mad are slightly assuaged by the sight of a family we meet on our way down off the low hill. They are making their way up to the top with all the ingredients of a good bar-becue (and this is 09.45 in the morning) including wok, wine, driftwood and wide-brimmed hats. Not that they are going to eat their hats, we presume. No – we presume that they are off to watch the eclipse from the top of little Orosay, and who can blame them. They'll probably sear themselves a nice vegetarian brunch. Certainly the tides are favourable for an extended stay. They'll know every blade of grass by the end of their sojourn. Sandy and I are just glad that we are not the only maddies about.

We turn now to head north for our long cycle up to Lochmaddy. Immediately the wind is there to meet us.

Despite health warnings about looking at the sun from sources like the Government, the BBC and Patrick Moore, in that order of increas-ing credulity, we are now stopping every five minutes to give the most ephemeral of glances at it through our cycling glasses to see if we can see the start of the eclipse. And we can. Round about four o' clock (if the sun were a clock face) a dark smudge is apparent. Fortunately we have brought the makings of a pin-hole camera with us (see, we *did* listen to dear old Patrick). This takes the resourceful form of two pieces of paper torn from my notebook, with a 3mm hole punched through by a pencil and held about thirty centimetres apart. To our surprise, indeed amazement – good on you Patrick - there is a fuzzy, but none-theless unmistakable image of the sun with a shadow lying across it. Each time we stop and look at it the shadow has moved. At its best, around 11.15, about seventy per cent of the sun's image is hidden – only the top crescent showing.

We look around to share the experience with others, but all we see are cows chewing the cud slowly in a completely unconcerned fashion (unless they are showing great restraint). The landscape about us is not exactly plunged into darkened gloom but there is certainly a bluish hue to the light now as if the sun has turned down its dimmer switch a couple of notches. This lasts for about fifteen minutes. The light is distinctly odd and all the colours around us have been toned down. We look for evidence of the animals in the fields acting in a bizarre fashion but all we see are sheep managing to get themselves on the wrong sides of fences and chickens running about aimlessly, and they do that anyway, eclipse or no eclipse. I eye Sandy surreptitiously to see if he has been adversely affected by this astronomical phenomenon. But he is cleaning cow shit off his legs and moaning about the wind, so I am reassured that all is normal here also.

We have to push on, we have been on the road for two hours and are still only three miles from our starting point. At this rate we'll get to Lochmaddy a week on Thursday.

The road is quiet and very straight with colourful meadows like an artist's palette still dominating either side. About twenty minutes up the road I stop again to bring out the pin-hole camera but our enthusiasm is now waning. We both recognise the symptoms – we have "eclipse-fatigue".

A bit further on we come to the birthplace in 1722 of Flora MacDonald, that Hebridean lass who was so instrumental in helping Bonnie Prince Charlie escape the English forces in the 1740s (there are still many Scots today who reckon she shouldn't have bothered). The most fascinating fact on the information board at the cairn is that when she died in 1790 on the island of Skye, three thousand mourners came to her funeral and three hundred gallons of whisky were drunk – that's more than three-quarters of a pint each! It must have been a riotous send-off. Who could ask for more?

The road on South Uist continues long and straight. The wind is light but unremitting. I'm cycling along with only the six middle gears working. I could get off every time I come to an incline and get my fingers covered in oil by changing the chain onto a smaller chain-ring, but why bother. Progress is fairly good despite these hindrances but the wind is beginning to get to Sandy a bit. The signs are there. Over the last few days I have observed that he goes storming ahead of me when amidst a personal battle with the elements which he is determined not to lose – and he never does. He is doing this now, gradually increasing the distance between us. There is another sign. He has started cursing at the sheep again. Poor innocent, black-faced, fattening lambs, and their 'glaikit' mothers, are subjected to his passing comments:

"Stupid sheep !" or "stupid ball of wool !" or, even worse, "Get off the road you daft animal." The degree of malice in his curses is directly proportional to the strength of the wind in his face. I, for one, don't blame him. At least he's not taking it out on me.

We stop at the roadside on Mointeach Mhor to reduce the weight of our packed lunches and study the map. It suddenly strikes me that for the first time ever I will be cycling from the bottom of an OS map to the top of it – a fact that I find rather disconcerting. Studying our route further I realise that our cycle today is so long it requires three OS maps to cover the route. Our lunch is all but gone and we are still only nine miles into our trek. We press on.

A few miles further, near the northern end of this predominantly Roman Catholic island, we see a stylish statue of Mary holding Jesus – strategically, or perhaps tactically, positioned on a hillside facing north to the predominantly Protestant North Uist. Soon we are on the ecumenical island of Benbecula – linked to South Uist by a causeway. After a brief roadside debate we are unanimous in agreeing that instead of continuing up the main road we will take another diversion, westwards along a B road, in order to enjoy a well deserved rest on a beach and to visit the airport at Baile Mhanaich. Although this adds a couple of miles to our journey it gives us a wonderful reprieve from the wind – if only for three or four miles. As we turn the corner just past Creagory there is that wonderful feeling of the wind pushing into your back, and the mileometer is soon reading twenty-two mph with the minimum of effort. We know that we will suffer for this later when we turn face into the wind past the airport but – what the hell.

Just after Borgh we reach the sand-dunes, the bikes are jettisoned and we spend a relaxing half an hour looking at the wonderful beach and watching a lovely young female jogger do her routine. She cycles up quite close to us on her bike and then runs out along the full mile and a half length of the white sands. In ten minutes she is a mere speck in the distance. Then the speck can be seen to turn around and come all the way back again. It is so nice to see someone else do all the hard work for a while. We watch in silence, munching on the remains of our packed lunch.

"Phew!" breathes Sandy. "I'm in a lather."

On again but only as far as the airport where we learn that the Glasgow bound plane is about to land in ten minutes. Time for a tea and a couple of tuna sandwiches – all this cycling is hungry work. We know that the next few miles will be difficult, so we procrastinate somewhat. The plane lands and we are startled by a tannoy announcement that "all unattended luggage will be taken away and destroyed". We suddenly realise that this refers to our bikes and attached panniers leaning "unattended" against the barrier outside. Why the announcer couldn't have ambled up to us and asked us to reunite ourselves with them we don't know – there are only four people in the airport lounge, one is a waitress and the other two are wearing cycle shorts.

On again, the wind really is on the nose now – not just on the nose but up it as well. Sandy's sheep cursing is getting louder, this despite the fact that the distance between him and me has lengthened to about a quarter of a mile. He raises himself off the saddle to leer menacingly at a roadside ewe.

"Baaah!" he screeches. To his horror she bawls back at him: "BAAAAAH!" A veritable ovine "to you too", if ever I heard one. We pass an aromatic bakery just as we are about to leave Benbecula upon another causeway and his integrity and dignity finally crack. He pulls up at the side of the road. "That does it – I'm going in here for a CAKE!"

"What kind of cake?" I enquire. " A birthday cake, an anniversary cake. . . ?"

"Any kind of cake." He disappears inside and then emerges empty-handed and somewhat meekly two minutes later. " I didn't see anything I fancied."

He mounts his bike and cycles off without a further word. The going is now a bit easier and the sheep are spared, for a while.

Across Grimsay, another tidal island and another causeway. It is a small low strip of land measuring three miles by two, sandwiched between Benbecula in the south and North Uist to the north. The road passes over a mile of its western extremity before crossing yet another causeway on to North Uist proper. As the road curves round gradually to the west we find our bikes pushing faster ahead with the wind again on our backs. At a road junction a bit further on we stop to look at the map. There are islands all around us although not obvious to the eye as they are all low-lying.

South of where we stand, on the OS map, there is a kilometre square containing what must vie as the kilometre square with the least features within it of any OS map; just a bit of blue for the sea, a smudge or two of buff for the sand and a minuscule wee island called Sromaigh – and that's it. But no, we are not heading for that one, further to the west is the very flat (so flat there are no contour lines on the map) five square miles of the tidal island of Baleshare. Another causeway links its east coast to Uist so we take a detour down to see it. The northern end is inhabited, indeed all the locals seem to be crossing over at the same time as us for a stream of cars overtakes us on the causeway. But the

110

southern end is marsh and sand-dune. We stay only long enough to record our momentous visit on film. No stunts this time – I get to stand quietly at the side of the road and pose proudly beside my bike.

After Baleshare we are on the final eight-mile stretch across North Uist to Lochmaddy. This section of road is mostly very good with long gently curving sections. Surprisingly the wind seems to have slackened a bit and we are making good progress, perhaps urged on by the thought of a hot bath and a cold beer. Sandy streaks well ahead of me as he senses the goal in sight and for a few miles I have the empty road to myself. I feel as though I am on one of those straight, flat, deserted American highways like you see in Cary Grant films. The odd car flies past as I pedal happily on at a good steady pace. By the time we get to Lochmaddy, cursing the unexpected final hill, there are fifty-seven miles on the computer – mostly into the wind and all with my six middle gears only. We are pleased with ourselves. We have done well. It's not every day one gets to cycle the Uists with no rain and an eclipse of the sun into the bargain.

Down at the pier, surveying the scenery around us, Sandy is still cursing however. "Look at that stupid cow!"

I look around but can see no cattle anywhere."Where?"

"There, on that yacht, that woman is feeding the sea-gulls with bread and now she's going to get her yacht all covered in guano." He didn't actually say 'guano'. But I know he's happy really.

As we tuck into a bar meal, fatigue is setting in. "Phew!" says Sandy, "I'm not going to eat another thing tonight."

We retire to a bar to watch Rangers playing Parma in a European Championship match. The locals are happy – the Glasgow team is winning. It might have been a different atmosphere if we were still in Lochboisdale watching this. I nip out at half-time to phone Clare. When I return Sandy is finishing off a half-time pie.

"It was free!" he exclaims.

It is an early night, forced on us by tiredness, in a village ebullient with Rangers' 2–0 victory.

Day Five = 57 miles

Total for five days = 134 miles

Day 6 – Berneray, Harris & Scalpay

B REAKFAST IS NOT GREAT. Our host manages to concoct scrambled eggs without using any eggs. Scrambled milk is not very nice. To compound matters neither the cycling shorts that I had washed last night nor the underpants that Sandy had laundered (he got a bit over-excited at Rangers' second goal) are dry. So we set off in a northerly direction with various multicoloured garments hanging from our pannier straps. If we had a rope we could have rigged up an entire washing-line between the bikes. At least my garment is black and merges imperceptibly with my black panniers but Sandy's are various dazzling shades of blue; he looks like a travelling underwear salesman – a sort of pedlar pedaller.

We are off to Berneray, a pleasant little island which sits a half-mile causeway-ride off the northern tip of North Uist. It is not to be confused with the Berneray near Mingulay which we sailed past earlier in the week. I have a good look at the map before we set off. It is rectangular in shape, about three miles by two miles with nearly all the settlements on the more irregular east coast. There are a couple of low hills and a centrally placed freshwater loch. But the most obvious feature is the three-mile beach that runs in a continuous strip forming the entire west and most of the north shore. This is separated from the rest of the island by a rich, mile-wide band of machair. There is time for a visit to the island before embarking on the main business of the day: catching the 12.05 ferry from North Uist to Harris. The earlier we go the longer we can enjoy the many pleasures of Berneray, should we find any.

For a change there is a slight tailwind, which is not only speeding us up but is also drying Sandy's underpants nicely. Apart from the wind it is a bit dull but not cold.

There is a lot of banter this morning, we seem to be right into the swing of things now and we cross the last ten miles of North Uist telling each other Billy Connolly stories, particularly the ones about under-wear – and there are a lot of those.

We come around a left hand bend and there, sitting on a fence post ten metres away, is a female merlin. It hurries off when it sees us and so commences yet another ornithological lesson. It is our second merlin of the trip but the best view I have ever had of one as they are normally seen darting low across moors, offering only the briefest of glimpses.

The causeway to Berneray only opened about a year ago and is a substantial affair – nicely complementing the surrounding landscape. We are on island number fourteen by 10.30 and anxious to see if the cafe is open. To our delight it is. I drag Sandy inside – he is complaining that my regular eating is causing havoc with his "dietary intake regime" or in other words that I am a bad influence on his eating habits. It doesn't seem to hold him back, however:

"I'll have the biggest bun you have and he'll have the one with the most icing on it," he instructs the lady serving us.

From the cafe we skirt the road around the eastern inhabited side of the island as far as it goes and then stroll down to the beach. It is spotlessly white and the turquoise sea belies the freezing temperature of the water. Some ruined cottages nearby take our attention for a while and then we set off to cycle across to the west coast. This proves impossible as the fertile machair on the western side of the island is being farmed and there is no obvious track across to the lengthy beach that lies on the far side. Never mind, we have a ferry to catch so we retrace our route back to Otternish on North Uist and board the ferry *Loch Bhrusda*.

This route links North Uist with Harris to the north by means of an almost impossibly complex route through and amongst numerous islands, rocks and submerged reefs. I hope the skipper knows what he is doing. No satellite navigation here – the skipper knows the route like the back of his hand and has to steer every inch of the way. It is a bit cold aboard and I spend most of the crossing below deck in the saloon. Sandy is up on top chatting to everyone – as he does. That is, after all, how the two of us met in the first place. The are some other cyclists aboard, including a husband and wife team in matching black and yellow gear on a tandem.

Looking back on the last couple of days I realise I have seen a different side to the Uists and Benbecula. I had visited them before but was always dashing between ferry terminals. This time, at the dilatory and lingering pace of the bicycle, I had seen much more and was consequently now coming away with a much more favourable impression. The sunshine helps to create a favourable impression of anywhere but I'll always remember in particular the unspoilt, bucolic beauty of the Uists and the charm and modesty of the people who live there.

Leverburgh on Harris, where the ferry docks, is a strangely attenuated village. The road leads up from the jetty and then turns westwards to cross a narrow strip of land, upon which most of the buildings are set, separating two small lochs, one a sea-loch and the other a fresh water loch. There is a cafe so we park the bikes outside and have a late lunch. By now you must be thinking we spend all day eating. Please don't be misled – we do.

I am particularly looking forward to the next leg of the journey around some of the most beautiful beaches in Scotland and then around the barren rocky mountains of southern Harris towards Tarbert. Sandy has done it before but it is all new to me.

Harris is big and seamlessly welded onto its even bigger neighbour, Lewis. Together they form the biggest Scottish island of all but geographically and historically, are really two separate islands. Lochs Seaforth and Resort coming in from either side almost make the separation a physical one but there is a ten mile wide band of mountainous bog between the heads of the two lochs. Whereas Lewis is boggy with hundreds of crofts and the largest town in the Western Isles, Stornoway, Harris is mountainous and 'beachy'. My distinction is, of course, a very general and personal one. My only previous visit to Harris was to the village of Tarbert and so I am very keen to get going to see all those wonderful beaches that people have been telling me about.

Most of the coastal road up ahead is flat but first we have to climb the fifty-one metres out of Glen Coishletter on the way out of Leverburgh. As we look back, away below us the couple on the tandem are just setting out from the pier. Their yellow and black outfits and flailing legs make them look like a pair of mating wasps. On the down-hill free-wheel I touch my highest speed of the trip so far – thirty-six miles per hour. The view now over the beach at Traigh Scarasta and the huge lump of rocky headland towering over it is simply wonderful. Here the beach is two miles long and two miles wide; we head for the dunes to ogle at it. I have to give a personal opinion now.

For my money the loveliest beach in the Inner Hebrides is Kiloran Bay on Colonsay, but for the Outer Isles then Scarasta Beach takes the biscuit, and what a double-thickness-chocolate-cookie it is! But then again there are lots of beaches I have not visited yet.

Further on there are more beaches, all of golden sand and I'm determined to have a paddle on one of them. At Traigh Lar, four miles further on, we stop again and off come the shoes and socks for a soothing, albeit freezing, paddle in what is effectively the Atlantic Ocean. It is a paddle cut short, for rain drops are beginning to descend upon us – the first rain we have seen this week so far. We have a steep climb ahead of us now over the hills above Tarbert and we fear it is going to be a wet one. Sandy zooms on ahead – what's new – while I stop to make some adjustments before the start of the climb. The water-proofs go on, bags are sealed up and zips are pulled home. A chap in tailored shorts and a pullover cycles down the hill towards me from the opposite direction.

"That's sensible," he says pointing at my legs, "long cycling trousers."

"Yes," I smugly reply, "I washed my cycling shorts this morning and they're still wet."

"That's nothing," he adds and gesticulates back up the hill. "I've just passed some clown up there who has his knickers hanging off the end of his bike!"

A bit further on, with Sandy just a red and blue blob half a mile ahead of me, starting his inevitable personal battle with the steep incline, I pause at a lay-by and a small Fiat pulls up where I stand. Out of the car comes a young woman who has also stopped to ogle at the wonderful beaches. Having a discerning ear I deduce from her accent that she is Australian. Her name is Cindy and we swap notes about our respective trips. It transpires that she will be on the same early morning sailing as us out of Tarbert tomorrow. I bid her "g'day" and strain on up the start of the big hill.

It is actually not too bad a climb. It's certainly steep in bits and I am definitely beginning to get wet as the rain becomes more incessant but I cannot say that I am not enjoying it. What keeps you going in moments of hard work like this is the thought of a great downhill ride to follow and a warm bath in the hotel once it is all over.

Sandy goes at a different pace from me as we agreed earlier to tackle the hill at our own rate and rhythm. This turns out to be a good idea as basically I cannot keep up with him without running the risk of putting myself into a coronary care unit. He races at the hill with his usual vengeance and naturally he is at the top waiting for me when I come along five minutes behind him.

The scenery up here is wild. This part of Harris seems to consist of nothing but boulder-strewn moorland, made bleaker now by the driving rain.

"Beware this downhill – it is very steep in places," Sandy warns.

I take his advice and certainly there are bits where my rear brake is having no effect at all in slowing me down. Fortunately my front brake still seems to be gripping – for the meantime. We freewheel at a safe distance from each other all the way to Tarbert – about four miles down-hill. When we arrive, a little after 16.00, we are both completely soaked, including socks and underwear (I can only speak for myself on this matter), more from the spray coming off the tyres than the actual rain. I have never felt so wet.

We check into the hotel and squelch past the receptionist on our way up to our room where Sandy immediately reaches into his panniers for two tiny glasses and a small bottle of malt.

"We deserve this," he says and he is right. I have no intention of arguing with him.

The rain is obviously on for the rest of the day, which puts paid to a visit to the island of Scalpay, now linked to Harris by a bridge. We had intended going there, a fourteen-mile round trip, after arriving at Tarbert but the prospect of a hot bath and a change of clothes is too tempting.

115

Sandy quickly locks himself in the bathroom while I sit and shiver in a chair. He has looked forward to this for hours and he drew the lucky straw to see who had the bath first. Steam is soon curling out from under the door and from the other side of it come ecstatic utterances like:

"WHAT a fabulous bath !" and "It's so big I'm floating" and then "I'm like a lobster" and finally "I'm in a lather!"

Once bathed and changed, however, Sandy and I are sitting looking at each other from the opposite sides of the room.

"Well – as I see it...." Sandy starts.

"Yes?" I wonder what is coming.

He looks at his watch. It now has a veritable fog inside the glass which is gradually condensing into a puddle.

"As I see it – there are two things we can do."

"Right let's hear them!" I fear that something profane is brewing.

"It is 5.30pm – either we sit in the bar and drink beer, or we put all our wet things back on and cycle out to Scalpay."

"But that's mad," I reply.

"Yes – but we wanted to *do* Scalpay and the only way we are going to *do* it is if we put all our wet clothes back on again and head out there. We're going to get soaked anyway so why not. We'll be back by seven."

Most sensible people would happily take the first option, even if they didn't drink, and it is certainly tempting but the more I think about it the more I say to myself – what the hell! It's why we are doing all this cycling, isn't it ? To get to islands.

Ten minutes later we are outside, in the same wet cycle gear, wet socks and wet underwear and getting wetter by the second. It's totally mad, but then the whole trip is totally mad. I wouldn't know if you have ever put on saturated clothes and stepped outside into the pouring rain in them but, without going into too much detail, there are more fufilling pleasures to be had in life.

Why put the same wet gear on again? Well we only have two sets of dry clothes left and we need them for the last two days of our trip. Secondly there is no way we can dry two sets of clothes and shoes overnight and we don't want to carry their combined weight around. But most importantly of all, whatever we put on will be soaked within the first five minutes so it might as well be the saturated clothes we've just taken off.

Scalpay is six miles away over a convoluted road that rises and falls by thirty metres or so at a time. It will be like climbing the big hill we just did all over again – and that's just to get there. We will then have to cycle it all over again to get back – only this time we are wetter, more tired and the rain is now heavier than ever.

Five minutes on the road and I can hear Sandy muttering to himself: "Why don't I keep my big mouth shut?"

It is a hard cycle, the hardest so far, but it only takes half an hour to get to the new bridge over to Scalpay. Just as we have cycled up and dipped down for the last time we find that we have to cycle up the bridge now – they've put a hill on it as well !

I have been to Scalpay several times before. It is a little revelation of an island off the barren east coast of Harris. It is a small, substantially populated and prosperous looking island whose folk earn a living from lobster fishing and weaving. It comes as a bit of a surprise after the empty bleak atmosphere of its big sister Harris. Until a couple of years ago CalMac ran a ferry service from Harris but now, like Skye, there is a sleek new bridge linking Scalpay to the real world. Because I've seen most of the island before I am content to go no further than the harbour and let Sandy cycle on to see the rest of the island. He pedals off.

The place is deserted – not one single person to be seen. It is like one of those empty towns in SciFi films where everyone has been turned to dust by a virus or been scooped up into an alien spacecraft. The answer is simpler – the rain is now vertical and it has become quite cold. I sit on my bike at the pier waiting for Sandy to return. But I wait and I wait and am now beginning to shiver. Every movement I make sends trickles of icy water down my neck and my feet squelch so loudly I'm beginning to send echoes around the harbour walls. I slowly make my way back but as I look over my shoulder I see no sign of him. I try ringing my bell but it has seized up with moisture and only gives out an impotent little *ting*.

Eventually I cup my hands and bellow his name across the island. In the deadened peace of the deserted village my voice reverberates all around and even I am startled. But all that moves is a little ginger cat which eyes me suspiciously as it creeps past on its way to a nice dry shed. Maybe it's an alien. And then way below me I see a bike wheeling round past the harbour and stopping. He is obviously looking for me so I call again.

Now he's got the message and he cycles fast up the hill to join me.

"Have you seen the other side of the island ?" he asks excitedly.

"Yes," there is an air of deflation in my voice.

"It's exactly the same as this half," he chuckles and pedals off.

On the way back the rain is now really biting and on the downhill rides the raindrops are so painful in my eyes that I have to cycle with only one eye open and even that is all screwed up. So for comfort I open and close each eye alternatively with the result that the sheep think I am winking at them. To make matters worse our clothes and boots are now saturated, it's like cycling up a hill carrying a couple of gallons of water.

My odometer is also acting strangely. The read-out which tells me my cadence (the number of pedalling revolutions per minute – pretty useless information anyway) is giving me a series of figures between eighty and one hundred and sixty. What is particularly odd about this is that not only am I going downhill and therefore not pedalling at the time but that I disconnected the cadence sensor from the bike a couple of years ago !

The assault on the last summit is nearly a killer – there is no option, we just have to go on – but we make it. Back at the hotel at 19.20 the receptionist looks at us with mouth agape – aren't we the same two she saw trudge in soaked to the skin an hour and a half ago? Squelch squelch up the stairs, two more baths and the dry clothes back on again.

The island tally now stands at sixteen. Was it worth it, or was it a complete, miserable waste of time? Yes, it was worth it – but it's a close thing.

We now have a logistical problem for the morning. We have wet boots, wet fleeces and wet shorts, and we check out of the hotel to catch the next ferry at 07.00 tomorrow morning. However, it is amazing what a warm radiator, half of the Telegraph stuffed inside your boots and eight hours can do. We hope that they'll all be dry by the morning – if not we'll put the wet boots back on again as it is essential to keep our second set of footwear dry.

Dinner is a sizeable chunk of halibut washed down by a good New World Sauvignon Blanc and a couple of Islay malts. Don't let it be said that we are hard on ourselves all the time.

Day Six = 54 miles

Total for six days = 188 miles

DAY 7 – SKYE *(again)*, RAASAY & HOLOMAN ISLAND

IT IS AN EARLY START, 06.45 TO BE PRECISE. We requested an early morning call at reception last night but the receptionist had just smiled and given us an alarm clock. At least he had set it for us.

The reason for the early start is that our ship to Uig on Skye leaves at 07.30 and we simply have to be on it. We are turning the corner now and heading southwards to cycle over the big island over the next two days before catching our train home at Kyle of Lochalsh on the mainland. We are hoping that the wind will not be turning with us but will continue to blow from the north-east and make life a little easier. No such luck! It has swung to the south-west and we are going to get it on the nose yet again for all thirty miles of today's cycle. Why couldn't it have blown that way during the previous two days? At least the rain has stopped – the clouds have wrung themselves dry overnight.

Amazingly our clothes and boots are also dry. We quickly pack up our stuff and without breakfast (which is a real 'downer') head off to the pier a mile away to board the *Hebridean Isles*.

The ship is surprisingly busy and there is a fair old queue for bacon and eggs at the cafeteria. I join it but Sandy does without. On board we bump into Cindy, the Australian girl that I encountered on Harris yesterday. I make the introduction. As soon as she starts to speak, in what is now clearly an American accent, Sandy opens up with: "I thought you were Australian. . . ." This really puts me in it – for not only does she know that I have been telling him about her but it also proves that my judgement of accents is of a similar standing to my command of botany. I slink away, leaving them to discuss the delights of New England and give myself a personalised tour of my favourite CalMac ship.

She is a delight: ample deck space fore and aft and plenty of cosy corners where one can relax (I am talking about the *Hebridean Isles* by the way). I spend about three minutes sitting in each cosy corner and then head off to the restaurant for another cup of tea. What now? Another look over the bow, then a brief return to the rear deck to check from the wake that we are still sailing in a straight line. Sandy is still out on the starboard side talking to Cindy. They have now reached Hawaii by way of Texas, the Grand Canyon and North Dakota.

We cycle ashore at Uig where there is the usual hustle and bustle

119

associated with the arrival of a ferry. There is also a reasonable climb ahead of us. The road curves steadily up from the pier to the top of the cliff where the view of Uig Pier and the ferry way below is dramatic enough to make a stop to get the breath back mandatory. I am still struggling along with the use of only six gears at a time – but I'm ahead of my pal at this stage. At the top the road passes across the north-west of Skye through some lovely scenery of sea-lochs and distant mountains. The inclines now are easy enough but the wind in our faces is a bit of a pain. It has been in our faces for almost every mile we have done – and we have now clocked up two hundred of them.

Sandy is really sickened by this. Whenever we turn a corner to find the wind impeding us he starts to look menacingly again at the sheep at the side of the road and in the fields.

At Kensaleyre a squall suddenly blows up and rain starts to fall with a bit more perseverance. We take cover in a bus shelter which is very handily positioned at the side of the road. Where else? After five minutes it has dried up and we push on, taking a right off the main road on a route to Portree which looks more interesting and which avoids a one hundred and seventeen metre hill on the main road. This route may avoid the *big* hill but it is not without hills of its own.

We arrive at Portree at 11.30 and manage to dump the bikes and dive into a cafe just in time to escape another heavy shower of rain. We recharge the batteries on lentil soup and tomato sandwiches — we will need them for the section of road that lies ahead.

Looking around us, Skye and Portree in particular, is fairly buzzing with tourists. The difference here, as compared with the Western Isles, is that they are mostly foreign; French, Italians, Dutch and Germans seem to be the majority. A Dutch couple stagger into the cafe weighed down with huge rucksacks which have all sorts of accoutrements hanging from them. The poor girl is almost doubled up as her rucksack is bigger than she is. When she drops it into a corner of the cafe and walks to her table she is still doubled over. Looking outside to the panniers strapped to our bikes we really are travelling light in comparison, but then we don't have to cart our living quarters around. I imagine Sandy with a bath strapped to the back of his bike.

Our next island is Raasay, about fifteen miles down the road. As we will be passing our overnight hotel on the way we plan to check-in and jettison the bags. Sandy sees the frown on my face as I glance down the street towards the bookshop.

"What is it?"

"I don't have an OS map of Raasay."

"But we're only going to see a tiny bit of the island." He groans and follows me off down the street.

On the road again, with the latest purple addition to my OS map collection stuffed gently into one of the panniers. The going now is hard. The gradient out of Portree to the summit just three miles from Sligachan is not that high but it is constant. The considerable traffic is whizzing past our ears and the wind is now directly into our faces. This last factor makes it a slog and Sandy is competing in his personal battle like he has not had to compete so far. He pushes on ahead of me as we struggle on at our own rates. Each time I come to a bend I think that this must be the top, only to round the bend and realise that there is another half mile uphill stretch ahead. This goes on for mile after mile – seven miles of it in fact. It is the hardest part of the entire trip. The only ingredient missing that would make it hell is rain. Mercifully it stays away. When we reach the top Sandy jumps up and down like a madman and blasphemes a few times – it is entirely out of character and I feel that he has finally flipped. Even the downhill does not fully compensate us because the wind impedes our descent and there are bits on the last two miles to Sligachan where we still have to pedal.

At the hotel we deposit our stuff in our rooms and then head off to Sconser, three miles away, where we will catch the ferry to our next island – Raasay.

The ferry is a former Largs–Cumbrae vessel, the *Loch Striven*. It is the seventh and last ferry of our trip. The short hop over to Raasay takes fifteen minutes and we study the map to see where we can go during our visit to the island, which will last about two and a half hours.

Raasay is a long, narrow island, about twelve miles by two, tapering to a fine point at its northern end. This makes it similar in shape and size to Manhattan. There the resemblance dramatically ends. Only about one hundred and fifty people live on Raasay, most in the only village at Inverarish. On approaching Raasay it look as though it has a volcano but closer examination shows this to be the flat-topped hill Dun Caan which is the highest point on the island at four hundred and forty-three metres. The island is sheltered from the worst of the weather by the mountains of Skye to the west and this may account for the lush, mature woodland on the south-western corner. Most of the rest of Raasay, and its smaller northern neighbour Rona, is rough and hilly ground. The road north through Raasay runs for about twelve miles but looks very "up and down", in fact at one point it reaches two hundred and seven metres. After the slog we had today we want something easy. The hotel is just two miles up the road – that looks easy enough.

This is my first real visit to the island – I stepped ashore from the ferry in 1993 and stepped back on board again – not that there was anything wrong with the island – I was just in a rush.

A couple of miles from the pier we come to the village of Inverarish and the size of it takes me by surprise; there are two rows of attractive terraced houses opposite a children's playpark which sports a sign saying, "Please do not use these playing-fields on a Sunday." No work or play is allowed on Raasay on the Sabbath.

121

We find the hotel, set amongst some attractive woodland. Compared with most of its big neighbour, Skye, Raasay seems lush and verdant. To our delight the hotel is open and we imbibe a glass of whatever is on offer while chatting to the friendly hotelier. It turns out that the owner knows several of Sandy's past teaching colleagues and they spend twenty minutes or so throwing names at each other.

"Dougie McPhee – oh he was a cantankerous old fart." That kind of thing. Sandy glances at a certificate on the wall and spots another name he recognises. "And Jimmy McBride, he was another pain."

The hotelier looks puzzled. "But that's *me*."

Sandy gets out of it slickly. "Oh I must be thinking of another Jimmy McBride." We drink up quickly and take our leave.

We head further up the road. Past Oskaig I nod ahead towards a little island left behind by the tide. Sandy reads my mind and shakes his head in silence.

"I'm not going any further than that island there," I reassure him.

Sandy nods towards a wooden telegraph pole just ahead. "And I'm not going any further than that pole there." There is a finality in his voice that makes me realise he is serious so I do not try to persuade him to go any further. His psychological battle with that hill this afternoon has left him traumatised. He throws his bike down at the side of the road and I pedal on ahead, alone.

A mile further on I stop on the road above the little island and look at my map. It is called Holoman Island. I wonder who Holoman was ? I sit and stare at it pensively for what must be about three minutes. This is it. The end of the line. Our trip ends tomorrow and we shall be going home on the train. From Barra and Mingulay to Skye and Raasay – what a wonderful week it has been. Holoman Island is, however, an island too far. There are only forty-five minutes left before our ferry leaves to take us back to Skye and I am not going to bother trying to claim it as yet another island. I turn back and find Sandy sitting on the grass beside his bike. He looks up at me, looks at Holoman Island and gets to his feet at such a speed that I am startled.

"Right let's do it then – you're not going to claim another island without me !"

"I wasn't going to bother..."

"Yes but you want to so let's go – what the hell is it called anyway?"

So we cycle back up the road I have just come down, Sandy pedalling away magnanimously, and yet, a hundred metres along the road he is muttering to himself again. We deposit the bikes at the top of a dirt track which leads down to the water's edge adjacent to Holoman Island. It only takes us five minutes to scramble across the boulder-strewn beach from which the tide has timeously parted. (Strangely, at all the tidal islands we have visited the tide has always been just right when we got there.)

Holoman is about a couple of acres of grass which falls away to a surprisingly steep cliff edge on the seaward side. Sandy points out a honeysuckle bush growing out from the rocky cliff face.

"There, are you happy now?" He chuckles at me. It is our eighteenth island – but we cannot hang about. We have just twenty-five minutes before our ferry leaves – and that's five miles away.

We stumble back across the slippery rocks to Raasay proper and by the time we reach our bikes there are only eighteen minutes left.

"Are you sure this is the last ferry, Stuart?" I assure him it is and we race off as fast as we can, with the wind in our faces, back to the ferry slipway. Racing through Inverarish at breakneck speed I glance constantly at my watch – hoping that the time will pass more slowly and the ferry will not leave early. We get to the jetty, puffing and panting and with our legs aching with two minutes to spare – and the ferry leaves on time. Sandy wipes his brow – and only then do I tell him that there is actually another ferry tonight after this one.

Back at our Skye hotel we celebrate our last night with some Real Ale – the first we have discovered on our route. There is nothing else to do in any case, outside the air is thick with clouds of fierce midges and some people are walking around with mosquito nets over their heads. One chap has a home-made one cut out from a pair of tights – he looks as though he is heading off to rob the local mobile bank.

I have noticed that Skye seems to attract the weirdest looking tourists – ourselves excluded of course. Apart from the chap with the tights over his head there are one or two young baldy types (imagine what the midges make of that) and a lot of funny hats. Most can be typed into three main categories.

There are the bikers, mostly from the Continent, with leather gear and very smart, expensive-looking bikes. Then the serious hiker types laden down with rucksacks and waterproofs. Finally there are the hippie types, who travel light, usually just wearing an over-sized jumper and a long skirt (the men as well) and who seem to be having more fun than the rest of the others put together. Sandy and I are the serious cyclist types – with matted hair, sore bums and hundreds of midge bites on our legs.

Suitably sedated I fall asleep about midnight to the sound of Sandy snoring, and there are two other rooms between his and mine.

Day Seven = 44 miles

Total for seven days = 232 miles

DAY 8 – EILEAN BAN

SITTING AT BREAKFAST WE ARE LOOKING AHEAD to the last bit of cycling of the trip with a feeling of dread. The reason is only the thickness of a sheet of glass away on the other side of the dining-room window. I have never seen so many midges. There are squadrons of them flying around outside, and even some inside, in belligerent attitude, just waiting for us to finish breakfast and dare to go outside to our bikes. When we do venture out to attach the panniers to our machines it is done in record time as it is a painful experience. To my undisguised joy, for the first time, they now seem to prefer Sandy to me. The only way to escape them is to cycle fast.

We have to cycle fast in any case for we only have two and a half hours to get to the railway station at Kyle of Lochalsh, and that is twenty-eight miles away. But for once, to our delight, to our heavenly delight, the wind is blowing from behind us and is helping to make the task a little easier. Past Sconser we turn off onto the shore road, principally to avoid the climb that the main road takes through the Red Cuillin. It is a beautiful road, empty of traffic, and the clear air of the early morning gives the sea and hills and woods around us a clarity that we have not seen so far on our journey. We fairly race on.

Upon Loch Ainort there is a fish farm and three men in small boats are spraying the tanks with powerful jets held waist high.

"I see they had the Real Ale as well last night," observes Sandy as he wipes another dozen midge corpses from his brow.

Further on, at the head of the loch, as we rejoin the main road, there is a sight to behold. A ewe and two of her offspring have wandered just a little too far out to munch at the lochside grass and found themselves stranded by the rising tide. Twenty metres of sea separate them from their pals and they stand silently on their tiny little grassy island looking forlornly back at them.

"Stupid sheep!" Says Sandy – but this time with justification. They will be able to rejoin their mates in about half an hour, we reckon, either that or they can try swimming.

Past Dunan the wind is really pushing us now and I get into my stride. Sandy eventually catches up with me just before Broadford. "Are you in a hurry?"

We stop at a shop in the village to stock up on drinks; I had forgotten to fill my water-bottle at Sligachan and now have a considerable thirst. The next section of road at Breakish is the most unpleasant we have encountered, for the road is narrow here and very busy with traffic heading for the Skye Bridge. One or two large lorries shave closely past us and a Spanish registered car gets so close to Sandy's panniers as it impatiently sneaks past him that he roars at it in anger (and in Spanish).

Tempers get raised again further on – this time mine. We stop on the Skye Bridge, with thirty minutes to spare before our train leaves at Kyle, and jump over the wall onto Eilean Ban.

This little island, our nineteenth and last, was the home of the author Gavin Maxwell (*Ring of Bright Water*) for a while in the 1960s. I have actually met a chap who owned it subsequently but now it is home to a major support of the Skye Bridge. We simply want to step on to it and have a quick, very quick, look at it. However we are met by a chap who waves his arms at us and politely tells us to clear off. "Have you not read the signs – you're not allowed to step onto the island."

We had seen no signs, there are none on our side of the road to read, but my blood boils when a stranger tells me I am not "allowed" to do anything (apart from commit murder or steal something or be generally naughty) especially when it comes to exploring a small patch of my own country. After a few words, much to Sandy's bemusement, it transpires that the new owners of the island are a conservation body who want the island to regenerate without silly people like me trampling all over it. I see his point, and when the chap sees that I agree and realises that we are not going to steal any of the island or rip up any trees or anything like that he turns quite friendly and even offers to show us around.

"Sorry – we don't have time," I explain. "It was just meant to be a quick look."

"Get yourself a bigger sign," suggests Sandy as we head off along the last stretch of the bridge and the last mile into Kyle of Lochalsh. Eilean Ban should have read Eilean Banned, however the conservation idea is well meaning.

We make it to the train with twenty minutes to spare. We did not mean to cut it quite as fine, one puncture could have made the last bit of cycling too frenetic for comfort. But we left the hotel a bit later than we intended this morning – neither of us wanted to be the first to go outside on account of the midges.

We have made it: nineteen islands, two hundred and sixty miles and still on speaking terms with each other. What's more – Sandy points to a gull flying past and declares it a herring gull, and he's right !

There is just one final surprise – *Two train tickets to Glasgow costs £82!*

"I didn't realise the train was going to be steam-hauled," I remark to the conductor. Sandy is speechless. The cost of a seat on the train for a few hours is exactly the same as the cost of our Island Rover ticket which gave eight days worth of unlimited travel for us and our bikes on the Caledonian MacBrayne network.

It has been great: the scenery, the islands, the weather, the friendliness of the crews and the stupidity of the sheep.

We had no major problems or mishaps. I've carried my medical bag around with me and Sandy has had the ingratitude not to have a single headache, infected cut or bout of acute diarrhoea. We shake hands as a means of congratulating ourselves on our achievements.

Just think – if the *Pioneer*'s cruise from Largs had not been full on that fateful second day of our first trip I would not have sailed to Arran on the *Caledonian Isles* and we would never have met. That would have been a pity – but then again I could have got to spend longer in the bath.

In the course of the two trips I have reached thirty-four islands and cycled a grand total of five hundred and fifteen miles. The islands visited were a good sample of the islands of the west coast of Scotland although there are a number of glaring omissions: Tiree, Lewis and Iona, to name but three. These were omitted only because it was impossible to fit them into the two itineraries.

Perhaps this account of my journeys around and upon these islands will make you want to go there yourself. If you do – don't let anyone tell you that it always rains in the Western Isles. I don't believe them.

Day Eight = 28 miles

Total for eight days = 260 miles

DAY MILEAGE 1995

Day		
	1	48
	2	42
	3	44
	4	38
	5	28
	6	40
	7	15
total		255

ISLAND MILEAGE 1995

Bute	15
Arran	15
Gigha	9
Jura	17
Islay	7
Colonsay	0
Seil	12
Luing	1
Easdale	0
Lismore	10
Kerrera	0
Mull	41
Ulva	12
Gometra	0
Coll	15

DAY MILEAGE 1999

Day		
	1	15
	2	14
	3	25
	4	23
	5	57
	6	54
	7	44
	8	28
total		260

ISLAND MILEAGE 1999

Vatersay	7
Barra	20
Pabbay	0
Mingulay	0
Skye	85
Isleornsay	0
Eigg	9
South Uist	31
Orosay	0
Benbecula	12
Grimsay	1.5
Baleshare	1
North Uist	26
Berneray	8
Harris	34
Scalpay	2
Raasay	10
Holoman	0
Eilean Ban	0.5

VESSELS SAILED ON

1995

Juno
Waverley
Caledonian Isles
Loch Tarbert
Loch Ranza
Isle of Arran
Sound of Gigha
Belnahua
Easdale ferry
Eigg
Kerrera ferry
Isle of Mull
Ulva ferry
Lord of the Isles

1999

Clansman
Mingulay ferry
Lord of the Isles
Lochmor
Loch Bhrusda
Hebridean Isles
Loch Striven